Contents

Part 1: Introduction   *page* 5
  Biographical note   5
  The genesis of *To the Lighthouse*   7
  A note on the text   9

Part 2: Summaries   10
  A general summary   10
  Detailed summaries   11

Part 3: Commentary   41
  Point of view in *To the Lighthouse*   41
  Characters in the novel   45
  Symbolism   52

Part 4: Hints for study   59
  Is *To the Lighthouse* a novel?   59
  Plot in *To the Lighthouse*   60
  Characterisation   61
  Use of symbols   64

Part 5: Suggestions for further reading   68

The author of these notes   69

Part 1

Introduction

Biographical note

Virginia Woolf was born in London in 1882, youngest daughter of the large and talented Stephen family. Her father, Leslie Stephen, was a distinguished critic, biographer and philosopher, and one of the most influential figures in the literary world of late Victorian England. Among his most famous works are the *Dictionary of National Biography* and the *History of English Thought in the Eighteenth Century*. His first wife was a daughter of the novelist William Makepeace Thackery, who died after eight years of marriage leaving him with one daughter. His second wife was Mrs Julia Prinsep Jackson Duckworth, the beautiful widow of a barrister friend, who, in addition to having three children from her first marriage, bore Leslie Stephen four children: Vanessa, Thoby, Virginia and Adrian.

The Stephen family belonged to the upper-middle class which produced most of the influential thinkers and artists of the day. They frequently entertained the greatest writers and political figures of the time, who were attracted to their Hyde Park house by Leslie Stephen's reputation and by his wife's famous beauty. While still a young man, Stephen had abandoned a promising future as a Cambridge don because of his growing religious agnosticism; and this characteristic of intellectual and moral integrity was to become evident in his children, particularly Virginia. His extensive library was open to the children, and in later life Virginia recounted with gratitude how she had worked her way through this library and become acquainted with an unusually large number of English and classical works. For the first thirteen years of her life Virginia and the rest of the Stephen family spent their summer holidays in a house rented for the purpose in St Ives in Cornwall, and the rugged beauty of this coastal setting seems to have haunted her adult imagination, reappearing in various guises in most of her novels. Although *To the Lighthouse* is set in Scotland, the atmosphere and detail of the Ramsay household owe much to her early, happy memories of St Ives.

The tranquillity of these early childhood days was shattered, however, by the sudden death of Virginia's mother in 1895 – an event that heralded a particularly bleak time in Virginia's life. She suffered a period of insanity after her mother's death and had scarcely recovered when her beloved half-sister, Stella Duckworth, died unexpectedly. These deaths plunged Leslie Stephen into an orgy of gloom, a gloom that clouded the existence of those who lived with him and persisted until his death in 1904, following a lengthy and painful illness.

After their father's death, the Stephen children moved to Bloomsbury and it was in a house in Gordon Square that Virginia Stephen made her first serious attempts at writing. While the bohemian ways of these financially-independent Stephen children shocked some older family friends such as the novelist Henry James, they quickly formed the nucleus of a brilliant young group of Cambridge graduates. In this socially casual but intellectually stimulating environment, Virginia pursued her literary interests, becoming a regular reviewer for the *Times Literary Supplement*, reading widely, beginning work on her first novel, *The Voyage Out*, and travelling abroad. Once more, however, her life was interrupted by sudden death, this time the death of her older brother Thoby, who died of typhoid on a trip to Greece in 1905.

In 1912 Virginia married Leonard Woolf, one of Thoby's Cambridge friends, who had served seven years in the Ceylon Civil Service and returned to England, critical of British politics and colonial policy. The marriage proved an extremely happy one. Leonard recognised his wife's extraordinary talents from the beginning and provided her with the encouragement and protection she needed to fulfil her literary promise. Leonard himself was a talented and versatile writer, and his work ranged from complex political tracts to novels and short stories.

Virginia Woolf's first novel, *The Voyage Out*, was published in 1915 and received encouraging reviews. Emboldened by this success, she soon began work on a second novel and continued to review books for the *Times Literary Supplement*. Although her work was interrupted by periods of physical and mental illness, she managed in her lifetime to produce nine novels, a number of short stories, and countless essays, reviews and pamphlets.

She was part of a group of people, now known collectively as the 'Bloomsbury Group', although it is doubtful if the members of that group would agree with their current depiction as a unified, homogenous circle. Early friends, mostly people who had been to Cambridge with her brother Thoby, included Lytton Strachey the historian, Maynard Keynes the economist, Clive Bell who was her brother-in-law and a celebrated art historian, E.M. Forster the novelist, and Roger Fry the artist and critic. This circle constantly expanded to include new friends, amongst whom are numbered T.S. Eliot, Katherine Mansfield, Elizabeth Bowen, Vita Sackville-West and her husband Sir Harold Nicholson. From Virginia Woolf's diaries and letters, as well as from the contemporary accounts of her friends and acquaintances, we know that she loved the company of others and was particularly devoted to children, especially to her sister Vanessa's sons and daughter.

In 1917 she and her husband founded the Hogarth Press, which developed from a small, second-hand printing press in their basement into one of the most successful and innovative publishing houses of its time. In addition to her literary interests, Virginia Woolf throughout her life was actively interested in the feminist question and two major essays, *A Room of One's Own* and *Three Guineas*, testify to her commitment. Although never as active as her husband in the politics of the British Labour party, she frequently accompanied him to political conferences and seems to have shared many of his political attitudes.

Her tragic suicide, in March 1941, came as a shock to her friends and family. She had just completed a first draft of *Between the Acts*, and the period following the completion of a novel was usually a time of deep depression for her. Added to her dissatisfaction with the novel was the terrible strain of the war; her London home had been destroyed by bombs and even the peace of the Sussex countryside where she lived was frequently disturbed by bombings and dogfights between the Royal Air Force and the German Luftwaffe. One morning in late March, she left home on her customary daily walk, filled the pockets of her coat with stones and drowned herself in the River Ouse.

The genesis of *To the Lighthouse*

The details of Virginia Woolf's biography are of more than usual interest when we come to a discussion of *To the Lighthouse*, for this novel, both in conception and execution, has extraordinarily close connections with Virginia Woolf's personal experience. Indeed, the very first reference to the novel in her diary makes this relationship quite clear:

> I'm now all on the strain with desire to stop journalism and get on to *To the Lighthouse*. This is going to be fairly short; to have father's character done complete in it; and mother's; and St Ives; and childhood; and all the usual things I try to put in – life, death, etc. But the centre is father's character, sitting in a boat, reciting We perished, each alone, while he crushes a dying mackerel.[1]

While the ties between a novelist's life and the world of her novels are complex and difficult to unravel, Virginia Woolf's biographical materials indicate unambiguously the closeness between the world of *To the Lighthouse* and her early childhood memories. When Vanessa,

[1] Virginia Woolf, *A Writer's Diary*, ed. Leonard Woolf, Hogarth Press, London, 1953, pp.76–7.

her sister, first read *To the Lighthouse*, she wrote to her:

> Anyhow it seemed to me that in the first part of the book you have given a portrait of mother which is more like her to me than anything I could ever have conceived of as possible. It is almost painful to have her so raised from the dead. You have made one feel the extraordinary beauty of her character, which must be the most difficult thing in the world to do. It was like meeting her again with oneself grown up and on equal terms and it seems to me the most astonishing feat of creation to have been able to see her in such a way. You have given father too I think as clearly but perhaps, I may be wrong, that isn't quite so difficult. There is more to catch hold of. Still it seems to me to be the only thing about him which ever gave a true idea. So you see as far as portrait painting goes you seem to me to be a supreme artist and it is so shattering to find oneself face to face with those two again that I can hardly consider anything else.[2]

We know from Virginia's reply[3] that she was delighted with this response but during that same month she wrote to two friends, Roger Fry[4] and Violet Dickinson[5], cautioning them against too literal an interpretation of the novel.

Without falling into this trap, it is useful to have some knowledge of the apparent similarities between the Ramsay family of *To the Lighthouse* and the Stephen family of Virginia Woolf's childhood. Like Leslie Stephen, Mr Ramsay is an eminent philosopher and man of letters who attracts a circle of friends and disciples. Again like Leslie Stephen, Mr Ramsay has a disconcerting habit of speaking aloud to himself and was, in his youth, an enthusiastic walker and mountaineer. The intellectual integrity of Mr Ramsay finds an echo in Leslie Stephen, as does Mr Ramsay's abruptness and impatience with lesser intellects.

Mr and Mrs Ramsay, like Leslie and Julia Stephen, are a happily-married couple, and their mutual love endures through the stresses of life with a large family. The beautiful, maternal Mrs Ramsay appears to correspond to Julia Stephen, who frequently sat for portraits and photographs by the most eminent artists of her day. From Noel Annan's biography of Sir Leslie Stephen[6] we know that Mrs Stephen had a need to surround herself with dependent people and Leslie Stephen fulfilled this need, relying upon her heavily to fill his own needs, real and imagined. This moral ambivalence is part of Mrs Ramsay's character

---

[2]Virginia Woolf, *A Change of Perspective: the Letters of Virginia Woolf 1923–1928*, ed. Nigel Nicolson, Hogarth Press, London, 1977, p.572.
[3]ibid., p.379.
[4]ibid., p.385.
[5]ibid., p.389.
[6]See Noel Gilroy Annan, *Leslie Stephen: His Thought and Character in Relation to his Time*, MacGibbon and Kee, London, 1952.

in the novel, and Virginia Woolf depicts in her a woman whose maternal impulses lead to the creation of an atmosphere of warmth and creativity, while rashly interfering in the lives of others.

The setting of the novel, ostensibly the Hebrides, is clearly based on the Cornwall of Virginia Woolf's early childhood. While revising *To the Lighthouse* for publication, she revisited St Ives with her husband, and wrote to a friend: 'We look down into the heart of the Atlantic from our bedroom. All my facts about Lighthouses are wrong.'[7]

There are several obvious parallels between the Stephen family history and the incidents which threaten to overwhelm their fictional counterparts. Mrs Ramsay's untimely death corresponds to what is known of Mrs Stephen's death; Prue Ramsay's death in childbirth obviously echoes Stella Duckworth's death, at twenty-eight, three months after her wedding; Andrew's death in battle reflects the death from typhoid of Virginia Woolf's much-loved brother, Thoby.

A year after publication of *To the Lighthouse*, Virginia Woolf wrote in her diary:

> Father's birthday. He would have been 96, 96, yes, today; and could have been 96, like other people one has known: but mercifully was not. His life would have entirely ended mine. What would have happened? No writing, no books; – inconceivable.
>
> I used to think of him and mother daily; but writing the *Lighthouse* laid them in my mind. And now he comes back sometimes, but differently. (I believe this to be true – that I was obsessed by them both, unhealthily; and writing of them was a necessary act.)[8]

Clearly, the writing of *To the Lighthouse* sprang from an intense psychological need, but this novel is not simply of biographical interest. Through her extraordinary craftsmanship and vision, Virginia Woolf has transformed the materials of private, childhood memory into an artistic entity which can stand on its own, independent of explanation or annotation.

A note on the text

To the Lighthouse was first published by the Hogarth Press, London, on 5 May 1927. One of the most consistently successful of Virginia Woolf's novels, it has been translated into many languages and has gone into numerous editions. The page references which follow are to the Triad/Panther Books edition, St Albans, London, 1977.

[7] *A Change of Perspective: the Letters of Virginia Woolf 1923–1928*, p.310.
[8] *A Writer's Diary*, p.138.

Part 2

Summaries
of TO THE LIGHTHOUSE

A general summary

Even before she had set a single word of *To the Lighthouse* on paper, Virginia Woolf had a clear idea of the structure, content, theme and even the title of the novel, commenting in her diary:

> The word 'sentimental' sticks in my gizzard . . .
> But this theme may be sentimental; father and mother and child in the garden; the death; the sail to the Lighthouse. I think, though, that when I begin it I shall enrich it in all sorts of ways; thicken it; give it branches – roots which I do not perceive now. It might contain all characters boiled down; and childhood; and then this impersonal thing, which I'm dared to do by my friends, the flight of time and the consequent break of unity in my design. That passage (I conceive the book in 3 parts. 1. at the drawing room window; 2. seven years passed; 3. the voyage) interests me very much.[1]

The final version of the novel was indeed divided as she had envisaged: Part I, The Window; Part II, Time Passes; Part III, The Lighthouse.

In Part I of the novel, 'The Window', we are introduced to the Ramsay family and friends, holidaying for the summer on a remote and unparticularised Hebridean island. The action in this section takes place during a late September afternoon and evening. As well as introducing the main characters and symbols of the novel, this section presents the central narrative issue of the novel: whether or not an expedition to the local lighthouse will take place on the following day.

The second part of the novel, 'Time Passes', is a poetic, impressionistic depiction of the changes which befall the house and its inhabitants over a period of ten years. The war prevents the Ramsays from returning to the house and it falls to the mercy of natural forces, of weather, of the seasons, of night and day, of time itself. We learn from parenthetical statements scattered through the description of the house's disintegration that Mrs Ramsay has died, Andrew has been killed in the war, and Prue has died in childbirth. Towards the end of this section, however, the comic figure of Mrs McNab, the old woman who cleans the house, returns to the house to restore order in anticipation of a return visit by the Ramsays. The passage of time is presented

[1] *A Writer's Diary*, pp.80–1.

through the unfolding of key images rather than through the more orthodox method of chronological development, and this whole central section represents a technical *tour de force* by Virginia Woolf.

The third and final section of *To the Lighthouse*, 'The Lighthouse', depicts the return visit to the house by the remaining Ramsays and their long-delayed expedition to the lighthouse. Certain guests return with them, and the novel closes with the artistic triumph of Lily Briscoe, a visitor on the earlier occasion also. While Mr Ramsay and two of the children make their way to the lighthouse, Lily resumes work on a painting interrupted ten years earlier and as she does so, she has a fleeting vision which seems to bring into perspective the significance of past and present. The arrival of the Ramsays at the lighthouse coincides with the completion of Lily's picture, and each event adds a depth of symbolic meaning to the other, bringing all levels of the novel to a satisfying conclusion.

Detailed summaries

Part I, Section 1

This first section of the novel sets the scene for the book and introduces us to two of the main characters, Mr and Mrs Ramsay.

Mrs Ramsay sits with her young son James and knits a stocking for the son of the lighthouse keeper in anticipation of a visit to the lighthouse which the family has planned for the following day. Mr Ramsay intrudes upon this tranquil scene, pointing out that the weather is about to change and the forthcoming trip must be postponed. Despite Mrs Ramsay's attempts to placate James, Mr Ramsay continues to insist that they will be unable to visit the lighthouse, and he is joined by the unpleasant Mr Tansley, a guest and disciple of Mr Ramsay, who, to Mrs Ramsay's annoyance, takes his host's part in the argument. Despite her dislike of Tansley, Mrs Ramsay has an instinctive reverence for men and a strong desire to protect them, and is consequently disturbed by the hostile attitude to Tansley shown by her children, particularly her daughters. To compensate, she has made special efforts to be kind to him, inviting him to join her on an errand to the nearby town, in the course of which he has been captivated by her charm and beauty and has confided in her the pain of his past life and his hopes for the future.

In this opening section, Mrs Ramsay is established as a major narrative and symbolic centre in the novel. She is seated at the window, the link between the house and outdoors. It is to her that Mr Ramsay and Charles Tansley come. Her point of view is the dominant one, and we see the present and the past largely through her eyes. The two opening statements of the section establish two worlds of value in this novel: we see how Mrs Ramsay's desire to please her children blinds her to the threat of bad weather; and we see also her husband's rigorous, unswerving, but unsympathetic devotion to factual truth. While this first section is concerned with mundane events in a recognisable world (the trip to the lighthouse, Mrs Ramsay's knitting, the visit to the local town, the chitchat of everyday life) we are made aware of another reality beneath that surface, the reality experienced inwardly by the various characters as they go about their business in the world.

NOTES AND GLOSSARY:

clan:	family
ermine:	a small animal, whose fur is used to decorate the robes of the nobility
on the Bench:	an expression referring to a judge
odious:	hateful
Hebrides:	a group of remote islands off the coast of Scotland
admonished:	warned
Isle of Skye:	an island off the west coast of Scotland
Balliol:	a famous Oxford college
prolegomena:	preliminary remarks or dissertation
parasol:	small sun umbrella
somnolence:	drowsiness, sleepiness
lethargy:	apathetic state
Panama hat:	a light straw hat with a wide brim
Garter:	the highest order of British knighthood

Part I, Section 2

To Mrs Ramsay's annoyance, Tansley repeats his prediction that there will be no trip to the lighthouse on the following day. Ironically, Tansley has been trying to make this opinion more palatable in deference to Mrs Ramsay.

Part I, Section 3

Mrs Ramsay attempts to soothe young James's disappointment and helps him find suitable pictures in an old catalogue for his scrapbook. As she does so, she is partially aware of the reassuring sound of the waves in the distance, but as she becomes more aware of them, it seems to her that they have an ominous sound, warning of death and disintegration. She realises that her feeling of apprehension has been caused by the sudden silence of the people outside the house, a silence broken by the sound of her husband's voice declaiming Tennyson's poem 'The Charge of the Light Brigade'. The only other guest who can hear him is Lily Briscoe, standing at the edge of the lawn, painting.

NOTES AND GLOSSARY:
caustic: a substance that burns or corrodes
ephemeral: short-lived
'Stormed at with shot and shell': from Alfred, Lord Tennyson's (1809–
        92) poem, 'The Charge of the Light Brigade'

Part I, Section 4

As she paints, Lily is indeed aware of Mr Ramsay's recitation and, although embarrassed by his habit of reciting poetry aloud to himself, is relieved that he has not come to inspect her painting. She is joined by Mr Bankes, an old friend of Ramsay who, like Lily, is lodging in the nearby village. He invites her to join him in a stroll and as they take their customary walk around the garden, Mr Bankes thinks of Lily as a physically plain but sensible young woman, while Lily wonders why her paint-brush cannot capture the reality which her eyes see, and asks herself if it is possible ever to express fully the interior vision. They move through the garden, noticing that the air is getting cooler and together they gaze at the familiar seascape. Bankes is reminded of a younger Ramsay on a walking tour in Westmorland, admiring a hen and her chicks, and reflects on how their friendship has changed over the years, largely, Bankes feels, because of Mr Ramsay's domestic preoccupations. The sight of the hen and her chicks had been strangely prophetic and marked the end of their intimate friendship. He thinks of the numerous Ramsay children and the family's financial responsibilities and realises that, despite his sympathy for his friend, he also envies Ramsay his children. Lily reminds him about Ramsay's work and tries to imagine the nature of his philosophical work. She sees it as a scrubbed kitchen table lodged in a pear tree. Bankes continues to discuss Ramsay's achievements and as he does so, Lily mentally compares him to Ramsay, admiring his objectivity and his single-mindedness at the expense of their host. Even as she does so, however, she becomes aware of the complexity of Ramsay's character and his many praiseworthy qualities. Her train of thought is shattered by the sound of Jasper Ramsay's gun, shooting at a flock of starlings, and by the sudden appearance of Ramsay himself, who continues to recite his poetry.

In this section, the angle of vision has shifted from Mrs Ramsay at the window to Lily Briscoe as she stands before her easel on the lawn. We see Ramsay through Lily's eyes, an eccentric, selfish man. As Bankes and Lily stroll through the garden, this portrait of Ramsay is deepened and developed by Mr Bankes's recollection and his assessment of Ramsay's achievements. They return to the house, interrupting Mr Ramsay's privacy and back into Mrs Ramsay's line of vision.

NOTES AND GLOSSARY:

'Boldly we rode and well':	from 'The Charge of the Light Brigade'
Balaclava:	the Turkish plain on which a famous battle of the Crimean War took place in 1854, and the setting for 'The Charge of the Light Brigade'
jacmanna:	flowering plant
red hot pokers:	flowering plants, so-called because of their resemblance to a poker
brasiers:	iron baskets to hold burning charcoal or coal
Westmorland:	county in north-west England
Sweet Alice:	wild flower

Part I, Section 5

Mrs Ramsay, measuring the half-finished stocking against James, matchmakes between Lily and Mr Bankes, and looking around the room is suddenly struck by the shabbiness of the house. An expression of sadness steals over her face, emphasising her extraordinary beauty, a beauty which even Mr Bankes notices, despite the ordinariness of her dress and the banality of her domestic activities.

In this section Mrs Ramsay is presented mainly through the angle of vision of an unidentified narrator and through her own eyes. She is absorbed by domestic detail, the untidiness and shabbiness of the house, the Swiss maid's anguish on hearing her father has cancer, the length of the stocking she is knitting for the lighthouse keeper's son, her own son's restlessness. From the point of view of the external observer, however, she appears to be the epitome of sadness, and her beauty calls to mind old rumours about her ability to inspire men's love.

NOTES AND GLOSSARY:

The Graces:	three beautiful sister goddesses in Greek mythology
asphodel:	a kind of lily, associated in legend with gods and goddesses
goloshes:	rubber overshoes
idiosyncrasy:	a personal characteristic

Part I, Section 6

Mrs Ramsay becomes aware of her husband bearing down on her and as she chats with him about the visit to the lighthouse, they quarrel. He is deeply annoyed because she persists in her expectation that the excursion will take place, contrary to all the evidence. Repelled by his anger, Mrs Ramsay takes refuge in silence until her husband, ashamed, volunteers to ask the Coastguards about the weather. He leaves his wife and child and continues to pace up and down the terrace, his anger gradually subsiding. He acknowledges his dependence upon his wife, and his mind is free to return to the intellectual problems which had preoccupied him. In a series of images which portray him as a doomed and heroic leader, we are presented with yet another facet of Mr Ramsay's personality, and the image of the hero's wife used to describe Mrs Ramsay conveys something of the bonds which exist between them.

NOTES AND GLOSSARY:
irascibly: angrily

Part I, Section 7

Ignoring his son's mute animosity, Mr Ramsay returns to his wife for reassurance. The relationship between the two is sharply dramatised in this section, which shows how Ramsay depends on his wife's particular strength. The images used to convey the complexity of this relationship are extremely powerful: the male is represented by the 'beak of brass' and a scimitar: the female by a fountain and a flowering fruit tree.

Having provided the reassurance needed by her husband, Mrs Ramsay turns her attention to her son, but is aware of a feeling of exhaustion and disgust with Ramsay because he has shown his need of her. Mr Carmichael, the old and disreputable poet who is staying with them, shuffles past, forcibly reminding her of the inadequacy of all human relationships.

Part I, Section 8

Accustomed to having people trust her and confide in her, Mrs Ramsay feels Carmichael's reserve is a personal insult. She blames his coldness, however, on his wife, who has treated him badly and, she feels, has given him a suspicious attitude towards women. Irritated by her failure to charm Carmichael, she continues to read the story of the Fisherman and his Wife to her young son.

Mr Ramsay pauses on the terrace to observe his wife and child at the window and is refreshed by the sight. His mind is occupied in working out the necessity for the existence of a working class, and the significance of great artists for such a class. His intellectual integrity obliges him to face these bleak questions squarely and it is this quality of honesty which has inspired the great affection and respect of his wife and friends. He turns from the impersonality of the sea and his philosophical quest and gazes again at his wife and son, reflecting that his domestic ties, however detrimental to his intellectual progress, have made him a happy man.

As she puts away her painting materials, Lily reflects on Mr Ramsay's difficult personality and on the demands he makes of his family.

This section explores more fully the complexity of Mrs Ramsay's maternal attitudes and suggests that, as well as having a positive aspect, her desire to help others and to be loved has its sinister side. The association of Mr Ramsay's intellectual musings with the bleak seascape further reinforces the impression the reader has of a courageous hero of the intellect. Through images and the juxtaposition of points of view, the complicated relationship between the two is described more fully.

NOTES AND GLOSSARY:

adamant:	an impenetrably hard substance
acrostics:	puzzles based on the letters of words
guise:	assumed appearance
intermittently:	stopping for a time
obsequiously:	in a servile manner
deprecate:	belittle
Locke:	John Locke (1632–1704), the eminent British philosopher, whose chief work is the *Essay Concerning Human Understanding* (1690)
Berkeley:	George Berkeley (1685–1753), the Irish philosopher, is remembered for his denial of the existence of matter. He argued that matter exists only through being perceived
Hume:	David Hume (1711–76), the Scottish philosopher, whose major work is the *Treatise of Human Nature* (1740)
come a cropper:	slang for to fall, to fail

Part I, Section 9

Lily and Mr Bankes discuss Ramsay's faults, but Lily defends him against Bankes's charge of hypocrisy. She is about to criticise

Mrs Ramsay when she glimpses an expression on Bankes's face as he watches her reading to her son at the window, and she is overwhelmed by Mrs Ramsay's ability to inspire love and admiration, even in a man like Bankes. She turns to her half-finished painting and feels keen disappointment because she has failed to capture the essence of her vision of Mrs Ramsay and James. She traces her ambivalent feelings about Mrs Ramsay to their source: her great love and admiration for the older woman, and her anger and exasperation at Mrs Ramsay's assumption that no woman can be happy or fulfilled unless she is married. She recalls moments when she has longed to be somehow united with Mrs Ramsay, but reflects that such intimacy is seldom possible in human relationships. Mr Bankes examines her painting and asks her to explain it. She replies that she is trying to express the essence of Mrs Ramsay and James rather than make realistic portraits of them, and is gratified by his interest. She explains how she must confront a particular technical problem in unifying the elements of her picture, and feels herself drawn to Bankes in a moment of unexpected intimacy which she believes has somehow been accomplished through the Ramsays.

The reader's perception of the Ramsays and their relationship is further developed by the reflections of Bankes and Lily. Lily's perception of her hostess brings together both the positive and negative aspects of Mrs Ramsay's character which have already been hinted at, and indicates the mixed emotions which Mrs Ramsay inspires in another woman. Lily's interest in her painting in this section balances the intensity of Mrs Ramsay's domestic and maternal concerns and Lily, insignificant and plain as she feels herself to be, is given through her artistic commitment a stature to counterbalance Mrs Ramsay. The section concludes with the intrusion of Cam the second youngest member of the family, as she dashes past.

NOTES AND GLOSSARY:

Carlyle: Thomas Carlyle (1795–1881), the eminent Victorian thinker and writer

Brompton Road: a street in London

Part I, Section 10

Heedless Cam becomes a focus of attention for the people on the lawn and Mrs Ramsay, who watches her from the window. Wondering about Cam's thoughts, she stops her daughter's flight and learns that her son Andrew and two young guests, Paul Rayley and Minta Doyle, have not yet returned from a trip to the seashore. As she continues to read the story of the Fisherman and his Wife, she wonders if her matchmaking between the two young people has worked, and if Minta has agreed to marry Paul. Her mind dwells on Minta's parents with some dislike, and we learn that Minta's mother has accused her of trying to steal her daughter's affections, an accusation vehemently denied by Mrs Ramsay, who admits to a desire to improve the world by changing such things as hospitals and drains. She looks forward to more active involvement in such causes when her children are older, but quickly realises that she does not want them to change, fearing obscurely that the future holds some threat for them. Her husband cannot understand these fears, and gets angry when she speaks of them, but she knows that she will never be happier than now, while her children are still children and before time and death have had an opportunity to steal them from her. Acutely aware of the power of these destructive elements, she sees herself as a general making a truce with an enemy general, begging time, death and the forces of change which she believes are rampant in the world, to spare her family a while longer. Even marriage is over-shadowed by these forces and she feels vaguely guilty for having encouraged Paul and Minta. As she continues the story for James, she worries about the latecomers, fearing that some accident may have overtaken them, especially her son Andrew. The beam of the lighthouse shines through the gathering darkness, reassuring her with its familiarity, and she remembers James's disappointment about the postponed trip to the lighthouse.

Part I, Section 11

James has gone, leaving Mrs Ramsay alone with her knitting. She enters into a deeper level of thought than before, a level at which she finds the strength and resources to nourish and reassure those around her. The beam of the lighthouse enters her consciousness and she identifies that beam with herself. As she meditates, her face takes on a sad and stern aspect which makes her seem remote to her husband observing her as he walks up and down on the terrace outside the window. He is reluctant to break upon her thoughts because of this remoteness but she notices him and recognising his need, joins him on his walk.

Although this short section is almost static in terms of the narrative development of the novel, it is highly significant in the symbolic scheme. Mrs Ramsay is alone for the first time, and in the absence of the demands which are made upon her by other characters her mind can explore freely the territory beneath the day-to-day incidents and domestic worries which had previously occupied her. She allows her mind to drift idly and this new level of consciousness is identified with the steady stroke of the lighthouse as it cuts across the waves and the land, providing a beacon of safety against the threat of destruction and isolation hidden in the desolate seascape.

Part I, Section 12

Mr and Mrs Ramsay walk together through the garden, chatting amicably about trivial domestic matters. Neither mentions those problems and questions which had been absorbing them individually and Mrs Ramsay is struck by her husband's inability to see the things she sees and which, she feels, matter – the garden flowers, their eldest daughter's increasing beauty. Mr Ramsay in turn is mildly exasperated by his wife's tendency to exaggerate the truth and scolds her gently. Sensing their separation, Mr Ramsay pursues his memories of walking tours as a young man and thinks with slight regret of opportunities lost because of the responsibilities imposed by his family. Mrs Ramsay senses his melancholy but mistakes its cause and contradicts him. Even though he exasperates her she takes pride in his intellect which, she thinks, sets him apart from ordinary men and women. To please her, he pretends to admire the flowers and she catches a glimpse of Bankes and Lily, which reminds her of her match-making plans.

NOTES AND GLOSSARY:
'Best and brightest, come away!': from 'To Jane: The Invitation' a
    poem by Percy Bysshe Shelley (1792–1822)

Part I, Section 13

Lily and Bankes talk about the difference between great and ordinary men. Lily feels that her lack of knowledge of great painting is an advantage, since greatness has the effect of belittling her own artistic efforts. While they discuss the differences between the great and the average, Lily notices the Ramsays are watching their children playing cricket and for a moment they become for Lily a universal symbol of the unity of marriage. When Mrs Ramsay greets them, Lily is suddenly aware of her matchmaking intentions. A sense of mysterious beauty envelops the world but is disrupted by Prue Ramsay who accidentally runs into her parents, by Mr Ramsay's story about Hume and the old woman, and by Mrs Ramsay's anxieties about her missing children.

This section brings together the two couples who have hitherto been the main focus of the novel as they watch the children at cricket. Mrs Ramsay's irritating habit of managing other people's lives and Mr Ramsay's tendency towards pedantry are both dramatised, but so too is their symbolic quality as a universal expression of the unity of marriage. Ironically, at the very moment when they are perceived by Lily as symbolic, the Ramsays are spiritually distant from each other.

NOTES AND GLOSSARY:

Rembrandts:	paintings by the great Dutch artist Rembrandt van Rijn (1606–69)
Good Friday:	most solemn day in the Christian liturgy, celebrating Christ's crucifixion
Prado:	the famous art gallery in Madrid
Michael Angelo:	Michelangelo di Lodovico Buonarroti (1475–1564), great artist, sculptor, and poet of the Italian Renaissance
Giotto:	Giotto di Bodone (1267–1337), the celebrated Italian painter of the early Renaissance
Titian:	Tiziano Vercelli (*d.*1576), the famous seventeenth-century Italian painter
Darwin:	Charles Darwin (1809–82), the English zoologist and writer who formulated the controversial theory of evolution
ethereal:	light, airy, heavenly

Part I, Section 14

Nancy, the missing Ramsay girl, has reluctantly accompanied the other young people to the beach. She is particularly attracted to Minta, who seems to have access to a world unknown to Nancy. Her brother Andrew admires Minta for her lack of feminine silliness, but is amused by her irrational fear of bulls. The young people sing together as they walk to the beach.

Andrew is aware that he and Paul are behaving more boisterously than usual and their behaviour is connected with the presence of the two girls. When they reach the seashore he goes off on his own. Nancy does too and peers into rock pools, feeling strangely godlike in comparison to their inhabitants, but infinitesimal in comparison to the sea. Her sense of elation is broken when she encounters Paul and Minta kissing behind a rock, and she and her brother are unaccountably angry with each other because Paul and Minta's kiss has reminded them of their sexual differences.

On their way home, Minta is desolate to discover she has lost a brooch given to her by her grandmother. All search for it in vain. Paul promises himself he will return to look for it at dawn when the tide has receded, and if his search is unsuccessful he will buy her an even more beautiful replacement.

As they approach the town, Paul has an idyllic vision of their future life together and feels grateful to Mrs Ramsay for bringing them together.

NOTES AND GLOSSARY:
knickerbockers: loose-fitting breeches gathered in at the knee
leviathan: a fabulous sea monster
fissures: splits, narrow openings
weeping willow: a pliant-wooded tree that grows beside water
presentiment: vague expectation, foreboding

Part I, Section 15

Prue Ramsay tells her mother that Nancy has indeed accompanied the others on their expedition to the beach. The episode of Paul and Minta at the beach is framed by the question and answer in the garden, which ensures that Mrs Ramsay remains at the centre of the novel, despite her absence from the beach.

Part I, Section 16

In the company of her children, Jasper and Rose, Mrs Ramsay dresses for dinner. While the children choose the jewellery she will wear, her fears for the absent young people intensify. With her children she observes the antics of the rooks in the trees outside, particularly two she has named Joseph and Mary. Rose carefully chooses a necklace for her mother, and Mrs Ramsay reflects upon her daughter's great, wordless love and her own inability to return it fully. As she gently chides Jasper for shooting at the rooks, a commotion downstairs announces the return of the young people. Relieved and annoyed, she descends to greet them and to announce dinner.

NOTES AND GLOSSARY:
holocaust: burnt offering, wholesale disaster
antagonist: enemy

Part I, Section 17

Mrs Ramsay feels depressed as she surveys family and guests gathered round the dinner table; yet again she is obliged to muster her energies to create an ambiance in which her guests can enjoy themselves.

Her pity for the childless widower Bankes stimulates her, and Lily, who respects and admires Bankes, notices this surge of vigour with amused contempt. Tansley, the awkward young academic, is feeling uncomfortable in this unfamiliar social situation and resents the social conventions to which he must defer. Mrs Ramsay attempts to put him at his ease with a conventional remark, but he responds with anger to what he senses is her patronising attitude. He blames women for forcing men to conform to social trivia, and maliciously reminds her that the trip to the lighthouse will be postponed.

Sensing his intent, Lily contemplates Tansley's unpleasant characteristics and again feels irritated by his dismissal of women's achievements. He responds rudely to an innocuous remark of hers, resentfully remembering his own impoverished past then, ashamed of the uncouth impression he is making on the others, he turns to Mrs Ramsay for reassurance. She and Bankes, however, are chatting about the disintegration of friendships, and Bankes privately congratulates himself on his wide circle of acquaintances. Disliking meals with others and irritated by the constant interruptions, he acknowledges that his friendship with the Ramsays obliges him, against his wishes, to join them at table. When he realises that this train of thought is treacherous, he feels contrite. To cover their awkwardness, Bankes and Mrs Ramsay exchange social banalities and Tansley, hearing them but not understanding the reason, is angered by their insincerity. He condemns Ramsay for allowing himself to be trapped by his wife in domestic and social triviality.

Despite her dislike of Tansley, Lily recognises his unhappiness and tries to soothe him. His response to her reveals a sense of inferiority based on his unhappy childhood. Although Lily is increasingly repelled by Tansley's attitude she responds to a wordless appeal from her hostess and continues her efforts. Reassured by Lily, Tansley recounts some anecdotes from his past, and Lily is rewarded by her consciousness of Mrs Ramsay's gratitude. She is, however, disturbed by the element of hypocrisy in her behaviour, and tries to evade her guilt by thinking of her unfinished painting.

Satisfied that all is well at table, Mrs Ramsay thinks about her former friends – the subjects of her recent conversation with Bankes. The men discuss politics, but Lily and Mrs Ramsay sense that beneath the surface something has gone wrong. Bankes, watching Tansley, acknowledges his dislike of the younger man, whose attitude indicates contempt for the achievements of Bankes's generation. But despite this dislike, Bankes judiciously reminds himself of Tansley's admirable qualities and admits that many of the younger man's arguments are valid.

As Mrs Ramsay waits for her husband to speak, she suddenly realises how strong her admiration for him is. Mr Carmichael has asked for a second helping of soup, and she observes that her husband, who hates to be delayed, is angry. She contrasts his moodiness with Carmichael's composure. She respects Carmichael for his poetic ability and for his affection for her son Andrew, though she is fully aware that Carmichael does not care for her.

The newly-lit candles reveal the beauty of the table's centre-piece of fruit, contrived by Rose. The candlelight and the centre-piece impose a unity upon the group around the table and appear to separate them from the dark outside world. They are conscious of being set apart, as if on an island, in common cause against the dark forces represented by the sea. Lily associates this moment of vision with her earlier perception of the Ramsays as they stood together on the lawn.

Minta and Paul enter, with the maid who is carrying the main course; and Minta recounts the loss of her brooch. As Minta flirts with Ramsay she becomes aware of her own beauty, and Mrs Ramsay realises that she and Paul are engaged. Mr Ramsay's obvious enjoyment of Minta's company causes Mrs Ramsay a jealous pang. She reflects on her husband's continued attractiveness and her own fading beauty. She turns to Paul, realising that she prefers stupid but charming young men to clever ones; and as they talk she observes Paul's affection for Minta. As she speculates about their future together the maid serves the entree, *Boeuf en Daube,* which is a success. Lily watches Mrs Ramsay relax, secure in the confidence of the young couple's affection, and Lily resents her dominion over them. She perceives that it is Mrs Ramsay's will which has brought Paul and Minta together, and she suddenly feels grey and inconspicuous beside Paul's radiant happiness as he promises to find Minta's brooch the next day. Desiring some share in the young people's radiance, she offers to accompany Paul on his search, but something in his reply reveals a latent ferocity which makes her glad she is unmarried. In the Ramsay's company, Lily becomes acutely aware of the complexity and contradictions of human experience.

While she listens to the conversation in an attempt to learn something about love, Lily watches Mrs Ramsay's family tease her as she lectures them about the English dairy system. Mrs Ramsay notices that Lily and Tansley have been excluded from this group because, she feels, they are unable to inspire love. She admires Lily, though she fears that no man (unless an older one like Bankes) will ever want to marry her. She plots to make a match between them. Fulfilled by the sense of unity around her table, she acknowledges to herself that her work as hostess creates something frail yet permanent, to defy the flux of life and change.

As the other guests discuss mathematics and the Waverley novels (topics she considers masculine), Mrs Ramsay notices Tansley's subdued anger and searches for its cause. She disengages her mind from

the conversation and enjoys a moment of peace, shattered by her awareness of a change in the atmosphere which has put her husband on the
defensive. Minta Doyle saves the situation by flirting with Ramsay,
and with mixed feelings of gratitude and irritation Mrs Ramsay turns
once more to Paul. As they talk, she admires the beauty of the arrange-
ment of fruit on the table, but even as she looks, someone takes a pear
and spoils its symmetry. Her eyes travel to her own children seated
around the table and sadly she wonders about their future, independent
of her. Prue, her eldest daughter, seems drawn to the radiance of passion surrounding Minta; but Mrs Ramsay wants more for her children
than the common human experiences. She realises that the dinner
party is drawing to a close and is suddenly aware that she likes Tansley
despite his awkwardness. Her husband is enjoying himself, and as the
dinner continues she allows her mind to drift with the current of the
poetry her husband is reciting. Ignoring the meaning of the words, she
delights in the music and as the guests continue the recitation together,
she feels that everything has finally fallen into place. She leaves the
dining table, acknowledging that this moment of completion is passing,
even as she recognises it.

Section 17 is the heart of the first part of *To the Lighthouse*, bringing
together family and guests on a literal level and many of the major
symbols and images of the novel on a poetic level. It represents the
summit of Mrs Ramsay's achievements as creator, mother and hostess.
The setting of the dinner party, guests and family gathered around a
lighted table with Mrs Ramsay at its head, with the noise of the sea
and the threat of the darkness outside, has obvious symbolic as well as
narrative significance. Through the direct and indirect interventions of
Mrs Ramsay, the individuals around the table are brought together in a
moment of unity, of friendship, of communion; which, although it will
pass in time, will survive in the memories of those present and constitute
a reality as complete and triumphant as a work of art.

NOTES AND GLOSSARY:

meagre:	insufficient, scanty
punctiliously:	meticulously correctly
demeanour:	bearing, appearance, behaviour
smite:	strike
fogies:	old-fashioned fellows
Neptune:	god of the sea in classical mythology
Bacchus:	god of wine in classical mythology
Middlemarch:	a famous Victorian novel (1871–2), written by George Eliot, the pen name of Mary Ann Evans (1819–80)
to vail her crest:	to hide a distinguishing feature

Sir Walter: Sir Walter Scott (1771–1832), Scottish author and
        poet, author of the Waverley novels
'come out and climb the garden path . . .': from Charles Elton's
        poem of the same name

Part I, Section 18

Lily cannot understand Mrs Ramsay's departure but she notices that
the dinner party disintegrates without her. Walking towards the
nursery, Mrs Ramsay reflects upon the moment of complete happiness
she had felt during dinner and her awareness of having accomplished
something important in bringing together the different people who
were present. She knows she has created a memory which will draw
them together in time to come, and will become part of Paul and
Minta's marriage. When she finds out that the two small children are
still awake, she is annoyed to discover that the boar's skull Edward
had found earlier is in the nursery and disturbing the children. She
tries in vain to console Cam and finally drapes her green shawl over the
skull, telling Cam that the terrible skull has been transformed into a
mountain and a garden. As she tells her stories, Cam falls asleep, and
Mrs Ramsay then turns to James, promising that they will visit the lighthouse as soon as the weather is suitable.

Quietly leaving the children's room, she worries that Tansley, in the
room above, will throw books on his floor and waken the children;
and she thinks about the paradox of his pleasant and unpleasant
qualities. She turns at the window to see the harvest moon, and those
outside see her figure. Prue particularly is overwhelmed by her
mother's presence. The security her mother bestows allows Prue to
become childlike again and she proposes that they go to the beach to
watch the sea. Suddenly gay, Mrs Ramsay encourages them, and when
she asks the time she is impressed by Paul's gold watch in its wash-
leather bag, which seems a happy omen for Paul and Minta's marriage.
Satisfied, she joins her husband.

Part I, Section 19

As she knits the stocking, Mrs Ramsay watches her husband reading
and when she understands he is reading one of Sir Walter Scott's
novels, she instinctively appreciates that her husband is worried lest his
work, like Scott's, will be forgotten. She is, however, reassured by his
expression of enjoyment.

Although she cannot fully comprehend her husband's desire for
immortality, she loves and admires him. Her mind drifts back to the
poem they had recited at dinner, and she reaches for a poetry book.

She reads at random, not understanding many of the lines and comfortable in her awareness of Ramsay's presence.

Ramsay is invigorated by his reading and dismisses his earlier fears that, like Scott, he will be forgotten. Stifling the desire to complain to his wife that he is no longer admired by the young, he discovers tranquillity in watching her read. She lifts her head, as though asleep, and seems to ask not to be disturbed. She reads her poetry, enjoying fulfilment in a Shakespearean sonnet. Mr Ramsay is struck afresh by her great beauty.

When she has finished reading, Mrs Ramsay resumes her knitting and ponders over what has happened since she was last alone with her husband. Briefly they discuss Paul and Minta's engagement, and Mr Ramsay speculates on people's reasons for marrying. Mrs Ramsay is depressed by her husband's silence, which he breaks to remark that she will not finish her stocking for the next day. She agrees, aware of her husband's need for reassurance that she loves him, an admission she is reluctant to make. She turns to watch the lighthouse, knowing that her husband has admired her beauty and that he needs her. Smiling in the knowledge of her happiness, she tells her husband that his forecast for the next day's weather was correct; and husband and wife recognise in this simple statement the reassurance Mr Ramsay has been seeking.

This section, which concludes the first part of *To the Lighthouse*, provides a partial resolution to the conflicts between the Ramsays which have been so evident at the beginning of the novel. The identification of Mrs Ramsay with the lighthouse beam is carried further here, and the juxtaposition of this light with her reassurance of Mr Ramsay provides a satisfactory ending for the first major movement of the novel.

Part II, Section 1

The guests prepare for bed and one by one extinguish the lamps, except Mr Carmichael who stays awake reading Virgil.

Part II, Section 2

As the lamps are extinguished the moon sinks and rain falls steadily upon the house. Darkness, like nothingness, invades the house and garden, and breezes sweep through, ruffling papers and walls, hinting ominously that the forces of nature and chaos will soon control the house and its inhabitants. Mr Carmichael stops reading and blows out his candle.

These two initial sections introduce the main theme of Part II of *To the Lighthouse*: the destruction of human achievements by time and uncontrolled nature. Section 2 concludes with the factual information that all the lights in the house have been extinguished, leaving the house and its inhabitants vulnerable to the onslaughts of darkness and the threats which that darkness symbolises. In these two sections we find also the combination of literal and metaphorical information which creates the impetus for the largely poetic sections which follow. The moon has sunk and a light rain is falling, and these details are juxtaposed in such a way as to suggest mental and spiritual darkness too. A shadowy spirit or *persona* embodying darkness begins to emerge from the details of these two sections; a *persona* which will be developed and made more specific as the 'Time Passes' section progresses.

Part II, Section 3

That particular night passes, but is succeeded by others as winter comes and the family departs. The house and garden, symbols of man's vain desire to impose order on the chaos of life, are buffeted and attacked by rain and wind. The sea continues to advance and recede, an uncomfortable reminder of man's powerlessness against the forces of time and death that oppose his efforts to find order. Mrs Ramsay dies.

NOTES AND GLOSSARY:
indefatigable: tireless
helter skelter: disorderly, in confusion

Part II, Section 4

The house remains empty, and the invading wind plays havoc with forgotten clothes, sad reminders of the human life which has flourished there. The house acquires the sinister loveliness and peace of a place from which humans have withdrawn. The silence of the house is disturbed only by distant sounds: the creak of a board, the sound of Mrs Ramsay's shawl swaying in the wind. One day this desolation is broken by old Mrs McNab, the charwoman, who has come to prepare the house once more for the Ramsays.

NOTES AND GLOSSARY:
quiescence: silence, quiet

Part II, Section 5

As the old woman stumbles through the house, cleaning and singing, she feels exhausted and weary; but there is hope in her singing as well as sadness, and her presence in the house signals a more profound optimism than any lonely philosopher can realise. Unaware of great questions of existence and death, order and chaos, Mrs McNab gets on with her work and returns to the life and comforts of the village.

Part II, Section 6

Prue Ramsay, radiantly beautiful, is given in marriage by her father in May. Summer comes and its beauty suggests that, appearances to the contrary, life is good, happiness prevails and order triumphs. Prue Ramsay dies in an illness of pregnancy. During the summer the beams of the lighthouse pass through the house, like a loving caress. The light illuminates the triumph of chaos and untamed nature in the once orderly rooms. Dull ominous sounds echo through the house, almost dislodging Mrs Ramsay's shawl and disturbing glasses in the cupboard. Andrew Ramsay is killed in battle in France. Philosophers find no comfort in the familiarity and serenity of the seascapes, for there is something incongruous about their loveliness. Strange sights are observed which challenge the watchers' complacency. Observers are led to wonder about the relationship between man and nature, and to conclude that nature is completely uninterested in man, despite man's hopes and wishes; and the sight of nature in all its beauty becomes deeply disturbing. Carmichael produces a successful collection of poetry. People say that the war has revived interest in poetry.

NOTES AND GLOSSARY:
rent: torn
jocundity: jollity, merriment

Part II, Section 7

The empty house bears silent witness to the night storms and the terrifying sounds of the stormy sea, which seem to threaten the land. In spring flowers come, but the contrast between the bright spring days and the storm-torn nights seems to emphasise further man's impotence.

NOTES AND GLOSSARY:
amorphous: shapeless
wanton: playful, irresponsible

Part II, Section 8

Mrs McNab does not expect the Ramsays to return and, assuming the house will soon be sold, picks some flowers from the garden and leaves them on the table as she cleans. She surveys the damaged contents of the house and thinks of Mrs Ramsay who, she has learned, is dead. The grey cloak recalls memories of Mrs Ramsay's kindness to Mrs McNab; but the war has changed everything and now Mrs Ramsay, Prue and Andrew are dead. Prices have increased. Mrs McNab remembers Mrs Ramsay's generosity and imagines her as she once was, in the garden. She feels she is getting too old to look after the house and despairs of its condition. The boar's skull has become mouldy; there are rats; the rain has entered. She locks the house and leaves it to its silence.

NOTES AND GLOSSARY:

Michaelmas: period in autumn following the feast of St Michael (29 September)

Part II, Section 9

Now completely undisturbed, the decay of the house progresses rapidly. The garden invades it; rats destroy the interior; butterflies and swallows make their home there. Mrs McNab has abandoned it, since she has not heard from the Ramsays, and the place is now beyond her ability to care for it. Only the beam from the lighthouse visits the house faithfully, passing without emotion over the destruction within. The house seems on the verge of becoming an abandoned ruin when unexpectedly another force begins to work.

Mrs McNab returns with Mrs Bast to re-establish order in the house. The Ramsays plan to return and the two women gradually reclaim the house and its contents from the ravages of nature. Sometimes, during pauses in their work, Mrs McNab reminisces about the Ramsays' past life there. Reflecting that they will find the house much changed, Mrs Bast watches her son clear the garden.

Finally the house is cleared, and the sounds of the outside world filter back into it; though silence still holds sway at night. At last Lily and Mr Carmichael return.

Sections 3 to 9 represent the very heart of 'Time Passes'. Early readers of *To the Lighthouse* found this lyrical part of the novel quite puzzling and some, such as the novelist Arnold Bennett, actively disliked it[2]. Virginia Woolf had doubts about her ability to bring off the

[2]Bennett reviewed *To the Lighthouse* for the *Evening Standard*, 23 June 1927.

significant changes in tone, style and movement in this section. But despite the technical difficulties it may have posed, 'Time Passes' was central to her vision of the novel, and actively embodied the cosmic, non-human antagonist of the human characters.

The problems of presenting such forces in a literary form more used to portraying man and men in society were formidable, and 'Time Passes' (particularly these central sections) shows how complete was Virginia Woolf's mastery of this form. Sections 3 to 9 are the most abstract in the novel, but are framed by clearly delineated characters: Mr Carmichael at the beginning, and Lily Briscoe and Carmichael again at the end. The sinister forces of nature, time, darkness and cosmic chaos which threaten the human order symbolised by house and garden are firmly rooted in recognisable events taking place on the narrative level of the novel. The semi-comic figure of the old charwoman, Mrs McNab, had not appeared earlier in the novel, and this omission is vital for Virginia Woolf's literary strategy because this character can be drawn in outline rather than in the precise realistic detail that might otherwise interfere with the symbolic movement of these lyrical sections. This movement is not entirely unexpected since a strong undercurrent of symbolism has already made its presence felt beneath the more realistic opening sections of the novel; and it is this thread of symbolism which is brought into prominence in the sections under examination.

Part II, Section 10

Once more the house is filled with family and guests and as Lily falls asleep in her clean room, she hears outside her window the murmur of the sea, which seems to beg the guests to admire its beauty. As Mr Carmichael lifts his head from the book he is reading, he realises that little has changed in the years since his earlier visit.

As the guests sleep, the sounds of the sea, and later of the awakening world, soothe them. Lily awakens suddenly with the knowledge that she has at last returned.

Part III, Section 1

Seated alone at the breakfast table, Lily wonders at her feeling of strangeness in returning to the house. Mr Ramsay and the children have made confused plans to visit the lighthouse, and everybody seems afflicted by a similar sense of strangeness so that they cannot decide what to take with them. Her feeling intensifies, and she feels alien in the house now that Mrs Ramsay, Prue and Andrew are dead. Mr Ramsay passes her and she pretends to be absorbed in drinking her coffee, not wishing to confront his obvious unhappiness. She is confused by her feelings and searches for the familiar pattern in the tablecloth to reassure her. Then she remembers her unfinished painting and decides to complete it.

As she begins, Mr Ramsay approaches and fills her with unease. His unhappiness has communicated itself to everyone in the house, and their meal on the previous evening had been tense and sad. It was his decision to visit the lighthouse and he is forcing Cam and James to accompany him, against their wishes. In the unhappiness of the two children, Lily recognises the loss inflicted on them by their mother's death. She feels Mrs Ramsay would have been able to resolve these tensions.

Lily determinedly sets up her easel in an attempt to avoid conversation with Ramsay, but to no avail; his presence is unavoidable and it distracts her. Angrily she remembers how he exhausted his wife with constant demands for sympathy and attention, and she realises that she cannot replace Mrs Ramsay as his confidante. Unhappily aware of Mrs Ramsay's death, Lily finds her creativity has withered and she despises her attempts to paint. Deciding at least to finish what she has begun, she tries to recall a particular facial expression of Mrs Ramsay, an expression common to many women in moments of self-surrender, a sensation unknown to Lily.

Part III, Section 2

Ramsay notices Lily and remembers that he likes her and that his wife had also been fond of her. He approaches her, looking for sympathy, but Lily rebuffs his unspoken request. They speak casually about the trip to the lighthouse but Mr Ramsay's desire for sympathy intensifies, and he groans. He reminds Lily of his wife's previous plans to visit the lighthouse, but Lily feels oppressed by his overwhelming grief and selfishness. Their conversation is awkward, for Lily cannot think how to respond to him. She notices Mr Carmichael reading peacefully in a chair nearby, his very posture seeming to taunt Ramsay's misery. Lily's inability to cope with Mr Ramsay fills her with disgust and she compares herself unfavourably with Mrs Ramsay.

Cam and James join their father, and Ramsay makes one final effort to elicit her sympathy. In despair she admires his boots, and is astonished to discover that her casual remark has provided the required reassurance for he proceeds to lecture her on the superiority of his bootmaker and on his method of tying knots. Lily is suddenly overwhelmed by a feeling of sympathetic affection for him, and just as rapidly irritated by the late arrival of Cam and James who are reluctant to accompany him to the lighthouse. She associates her respect for

Mr Ramsay with his lifelong pursuit of truth, and recognises his loneliness since Mrs Ramsay's death.

The surface disharmony and chaos reflected in these two opening sections provide an eloquent commentary on the absence of Mrs Ramsay, whose presence had imposed order and tranquillity on the household. In her absence, Mr Ramsay's tyranny over the children and his demands for sympathy are uncontrolled and Lily and the children respond with anger and resentment. It is, however, clear from Lily's observation that 'there was no helping Mr Ramsay on the journey he was going' (p.145) that this chaos is the prelude to a new movement in the novel. The voyage to the lighthouse is to be a pilgrimage, as well as a geographical journey.

NOTES AND GLOSSARY:
primeval: of the first age of the world
decrepitude: weakness caused by age
pooh-poohed: ridiculed
a lion seeking whom he could devour: from the Bible, the First Epistle General of Peter 5:8 referring to the devil

---

Part III, Section 3

As she faces her unfinished painting, which seems to reproach her for her neglect, part of Lily's mind accompanies the Ramsays on their journey. She tries to recapture the vision which led her to begin the painting and as she starts, hesitantly, to paint, her creativity floods back. She realises that although her painting will never be particularly valuable to others, the struggle to paint truthfully is worth the effort; and immersed in her work and memories she becomes oblivious to her surroundings. She remembers fleetingly an encounter between Tansley and Mrs Ramsay, and Mrs Ramsay's ability to soothe Lily's irritation with Tansley – a talent which she now recognises is akin to artistic creativity, since Mrs Ramsay, like an artist, strove to discover something permanent in the flux of human experience. Lily realises that Mrs Ramsay's legacy to her is the knowledge that triumph over time is possible. Down in the bay, the Ramsays' boat sets off for the lighthouse.

The Ramsays' voyage is simultaneous with a growth of awareness in Lily; an inward voyage to her final vision. In this section Lily has recognised her own inadequacies in dealing with the emotions of others, particularly Mr Ramsay's. As the Ramsay boat sets off, Lily as outsider, as artist, struggles to express a vision that encompasses her subjectivity and objectivity: 'She felt curiously divided, as if one part of her were drawn out there' (p.146). Her courage in attempting to express her vision is connected, through the imagery, with Mr Ramsay's unflinchingly heroic search for truth and his leadership of the expedition to the lighthouse:

> One line placed on the canvas committed her to innumerable risks, to frequent and irrevocable decisions. All that in idea seemed simple became in practice immediately complex; as the waves shape themselves symmetrically from the cliff top, but to the swimmer among them are divided by steep gulfs, and foaming crests. Still the risk must be run; the mark made (p.147).

As Lily's hand fashions the first strokes which form a 'dancing, rhythmical movement' (p.148), a flood of memories, images and names is released in her mind. One such recollection is the moment at which she discovered a liking for Tansley, under Mrs Ramsay's influence, and she paints that experience into her picture in red and grey. As her mind traces her relationship with Mrs Ramsay and Mrs Ramsay's achievements, searching for the visual image from the present to express the reality of her perceptions, her eyes follow the progress of the boat to the lighthouse.

NOTES AND GLOSSARY:
consonance: harmony

Part III, Section 4

On board the small sailing boat, Cam and James are irritated with their father who has forced them to accompany him to the lighthouse against their will. They have a secret pact to oppose his tyranny. The breeze catches the sail and sends them on their way, and Ramsay relaxes while he chats with the boatman, Macalister. Macalister tells them of a recent shipwreck and rescue of local fishermen during a storm. Watching her father, Cam recognises his courage and manliness, but her new-found sympathy is destroyed by her recollection of the pact with James. As the breeze freshens, all three feel a surge of exhilaration and Mr Ramsay, pointing out their house to Cam, is immersed in memories of his life there with Mrs Ramsay.

Cam is outraged by her father's flagrant self-pity, but as the lighthouse comes into view she rejects her own memories to enjoy the present. Her father teases her because of her inability to distinguish the points of the compass. He forgets his grief as he reflects that vagueness seems to be an essential ingredient of feminine charm, and he remembers regretfully how he criticised his wife for her vagueness. He tries to make Cam smile at him, which disgusts James who sees it as yet another attempt to break the alliance against him. Cam is divided between her father's appeal for pity and her brother's ruthless determination, and she answers her father noncommittally. James suddenly sees something in his sister's face which he identifies with a dim memory of his mother. Cam struggles to be kind to Ramsay, but is paralysed by her loyalty to the fierce James. As the boatboy catches and guts a mackerel, she evades her emotional confusion by concentrating on the distant, dreamlike shoreline.

Section 3 had ended with Lily's awareness of the little boat, nosing its way through the other boats out of the harbour. In Section 4 we are in the boat with Ramsay, Cam and James. There is tension between Ramsay and his children who secretly hope the expedition will fail. This tension eases as the sails catch the breeze and Ramsay relaxes in the company of the old sailor. There is a symbolic parallel between the story of the three boats which were shipwrecked during the storm and the death of three of the Ramsay family in the ten-year interval between 'The Window' and 'The Lighthouse'. Cam's feelings towards her father begin to alter and as the island recedes further into the distance behind them, it becomes for Cam an image of the past and a cause for rejoicing. She feels she can now truly put the past behind her. The receding shoreline reminds her father of the past, but as he thinks nostalgically of his dead wife, he gradually becomes aware of the living Cam beside him in the boat, and of his egotism and tyranny in forcing the children to accompany him. With Cam, Mr Ramsay has advanced another stage on his inward journey.

NOTES AND GLOSSARY:
'But I beneath a rougher sea
Was whelmed in deeper gulfs than he': from 'The Castaway', a poem by
William Cowper (1731–1800)

Part III, Section 5

The sight of the distant boat reminds Lily of her difficulty in communicating with Mr Ramsay and in vain she summons the sleeping Carmichael to share with her a memory of the short-sighted Mrs Ramsay peering towards the sea. As Lily paints her way back into the picture, her mind follows the contradictions of Mrs Ramsay's character and her immersion in the ambiguous world of emotional intimacy. She thinks of Paul and Minta Rayley whose marriage has been a failure and represents the inadequacy of Mrs Ramsay's need to know and love people. Fleetingly triumphing over Mrs Ramsay, Lily is suddenly aware of an obstacle to her painting, a reminder that the living always enjoy a hollow victory over the dead. Mrs Ramsay's death has freed her from William Bankes and Lily wonders about

Mrs Ramsay's devotion to marriage. Abruptly, she is reminded of the
golden radiance that seemed to flow from Rayley on the evening of the
dinner party, and she retreats from its implications of power and
sexuality, consoling herself with the thought that the Rayley marriage
has turned out sordidly.

Lily prefers friendship to marriage. In her friendship with Bankes
she values the qualities of aloofness and personal privacy, qualities
which can be seen as directly contrary to Mrs Ramsay's characteristics.
She wishes that the sleeping Carmichael would resolve her uncertainty about human emotions but despairs at language's impotence
to communicate truth. A feeling of age and desolation chills her
and she silently appeals to Mrs Ramsay. She senses that Carmichael,
although asleep, has somehow understood everything and has
pointed to her painting in mute response: time, mortality and change
obliterate human personality, but art confers permanence. Bewildered
by these ideas, she calls aloud to Mrs Ramsay, tears rolling down her
face.

NOTES AND GLOSSARY:

evanescent:	quickly fading from sight
levy:	collection of tax, or compulsory payment
Hampton Court:	a palace near London built by Cardinal Wolsey (1475–1530) and given by him to Henry VIII
arabesques:	style of elaborate decoration with intertwined leaves

---

Part III, Section 6

The fisherman's boy mutilates a mackerel for bait and throws it, still
alive, back into the sea.

Part III, Section 7

There is no response to Lily's cry from either the living or the dead, and
in anguish and shame she sees herself as a pitiful old maid. Gradually
the pain ebbs, leaving in its place a mysterious relief, as though
Mrs Ramsay were beside her raising a wreath to her forehead. Lily
returns to the problems of her painting, her mind brimming with a
vision of Mrs Ramsay that had haunted her after Mrs Ramsay's death
but which was gradually eroded by time. Noticing the distant boat she
remembers her earlier denial of sympathy to Mr Ramsay. In the clear
morning light, Lily feels a mystical unity in the seascape and, hidden in
the haze, the lighthouse seems to her more remote and distant than
ever.

Part III, Section 8

Seen from the boat, the island seems serene and untroubled to Cam. The sailing boat is becalmed, half-way between the island and the lighthouse, and all landmarks are fixed. Mr Ramsay ignores this calm and continues to read, a gesture which James believes is hostile. He dreads his father's awareness of this stillness and the reprimand which will follow. He is filled with violent anger towards Ramsay, and identifies paternal oppression with the institutions of society, which he vows to destroy. Despite his hatred, James unwillingly recognises his kinship with his father and tries to call to mind how this hatred came into existence.

Through a haze of memory he recollects his first surge of hate when, as a child, he sat at his mother's knee and his father told them that the trip to the lighthouse would have to be postponed. Looking at the same lighthouse, James now sees it from a different angle and acknowledges the complexities and contradictions of reality. Anxiously anticipating his father's reprimand for allowing the boat to get becalmed, he remembers his mother and is overwhelmed with sorrow for the past and worry about the present. Suddenly, to James's relief, the sail fills and the boat moves again. Mr Ramsay shows no signs of having noticed the delay.

In this section James is the main focus of attention. At this symbolic point in the journey, becalmed temporarily half-way between island and lighthouse, James uncovers the source of his hatred for his father and recognises that it is not his father he hates, but his father's tyranny. His altered perception of the lighthouse from this new vantage point symbolises James's growing maturity and his ability to recognise the complexity of experience.

NOTES AND GLOSSARY:
plumb:	vertical, exact
impotent:	powerless
sovereign:	old British gold coin worth one pound
perambulator:	child's carriage

Part III, Section 9

The seascape fills Lily with a sense of infinity, of unity with the whole world.

NOTES AND GLOSSARY:
valediction: farewell

Part III, Section 10

As the sailing boat approaches the lighthouse, Cam is struck by its un-expected appearance and feels the exhilaration of freedom. The an-noyances of the journey disappear. She wonders if the old men, Bankes and Carmichael, can understand and interpret this sensation for her, and she sees her father not as the tyrant whom she and James have vowed to oppose, but as a wise and lovable man. She watches him read, and wonders about his thoughts and feelings. She feels secure in his company and makes up a story about escaping from a sinking ship. As the island becomes less distinct, she decides that a ship has sunk at that very spot, and recalls her father's favourite quotation from 'The Castaway', a poem by William Cowper, 'We perished, each alone'.

This section marks the climax of Cam's spiritual journey, a journey which has brought her face to face with her fears of death and destruc-tion (symbolised by the shipwreck) and the sadness of the past (symbolised by the distant island). She recognises that this new-found ability to confront the past and the reality of death owes something to the sense of security which her father's presence inspires, and she acknowledges his strength, heroism and tenderness, facets of his character which she had previously been reluctant to admit. This new perception of her father and of herself brings about a unity between them, expressed by Cam's unconscious repetition of her father's frequently-recited poem 'The Castaway'.

NOTES AND GLOSSARY:
mammoth: an extinct species of elephant
plover: shore bird

Part III, Section 11

As she watches the progress of the Ramsays' boat, Lily is perplexed by the question of physical and emotional distances, and the curious altera-tions in perspective produced by each. In the unreal tranquillity of early morning, she is aware of an extraordinary perception of reality, of a kind of awareness possible when daily routines are broken by an illness or a long journey. This new and profound perception of reality fulfils her and brings her thoughts into a new unity.

Then the wind freshens, the momentary perfection of the scene dis-appears, and mental discord returns. She is dissatisfied with her painting and unhappy at her inability to express her vision. Once more she has a sense that everything is happening for the first, or perhaps the last, time. She is aware that Carmichael is ageing but also that his poetry has conferred immortality on him. When he heard of Andrew's death in the war he is reputed to have lost his interest in life, and Lily wonders about the meaning of the phrase. Although she still does not understand Mr Carmichael in conventional ways, Lily is aware of another kind of empathy between them which springs from their common perception of a shared experience.

Carmichael did not like Mrs Ramsay, and Lily realises that others may have disliked her too, for a variety of reasons. Mrs Ramsay's perception of the world may have irritated others, as Charles Tansley's did. Lily wonders what has happened to Tansley, and remembers a bitter lecture she once heard him deliver on brotherly love. He had helped Mrs Ramsay to look for her spectacles. Lily ponders about people's inability to know others.

As these thoughts run through Lily's mind, she remembers Mrs Ramsay's gesture on hearing the waves, and remembers how Mr Ramsay went to her. She imagines the moment at which Mrs Ramsay agreed to marry him, and thinks about their marriage with its moments of intense unity and other moments of sharp discord. While much of this discord could be attributed to Mr Ramsay, whose stormy behaviour must be at least partly responsible for Mrs Ramsay's death, Lily recognises that however reluctant Mrs Ramsay was to forgive her husband, she always did so in the end, thereby restoring family harmony.

Lily is suddenly aware of a figure sitting in the drawing-room window. The triangular shadow cast by this figure completes Lily's artistic vision, and as she paints she becomes aware that the figure is Mrs Ramsay, knitting the familiar reddish-brown stocking. Desiring to share this vision, Lily walks past Carmichael, in the hope that Ramsay has returned.

In recognising the mystery and the worth of the Ramsays' marriage, Lily has finally approached the end of her inward journey. She challenges her previous prejudices about others, as well as challenging her own emotional aloofness. The triangular shadow cast by the figure at the window brings a quality to the present which makes it possible for Lily to complete her picture; but she needs to share that experience with another and instinctively turns to find Ramsay.

NOTES AND GLOSSARY:

plantains:	herbs
flagellating:	whipping
cosmogony:	idea of the universe
crinolines:	very wide skirts, a style popular during the Victorian era

Part III, Section 12

In the boat Mr Ramsay has almost finished reading, and James, observing his father's face against the lighthouse, realises that his father is getting old and becoming a physical embodiment of that loneliness which both father and son associate with truth. As they draw closer to the lighthouse it seems starker than before, and James recognises that this view of the lighthouse corresponds more closely to his perception of truth than the lighthouse seen from a greater distance.

Cam, too, watches her father, reflecting on his unawareness of his children's hostility. The island is now so distant that the house and its inhabitants are minute, so as to be almost without meaning. Drowsily Cam imagines the house and garden are disappearing, but her father arouses her from this daydream, pointing out that they have almost reached the lighthouse. They eat their lunch and Cam's wordless fears of disaster are calmed by the reassuring presence of her father. They pass the spot where the ship sank and the three men drowned, but to the children's surprise, Mr Ramsay makes no comment. Unexpectedly he praises James's steering, and his son is elated. Ramsay prepares to disembark and his children watch him. They wonder what he is thinking, but he gives no clue as he stands up and leaps lightly from boat to shore.

In this final stage of the journey to the lighthouse, the three Ramsay characters come to the end of their respective spiritual journeys. Her father's reassuring presence enables Cam to put the past and her fear of death into correct perspective. (Mrs Ramsay had earlier attempted to soothe Cam's fear of the skull by draping her shawl over it.) James recognises in the lighthouse a truth which he and his father share, and he comes to acknowledge that part of his own character which strongly resembles his father. The conclusion of Mr Ramsay's voyage is indicated in his symbolic gesture of looking back at the island with complete equanimity, a gesture which suggests that he has purged himself of the past:

Thus in complete readiness to land he sat looking back at the island. With his long-sighted eyes perhaps he could see the dwindled leaf-like shape standing on end on a plate of gold quite clearly . . . They watched him, both of them, sitting bare-headed with his parcel on his knee staring and staring at the frail blue shape which seemed like the vapour of something that had burnt itself away (p.190).

NOTES AND GLOSSARY:
censer: incense-burning vessel

Part III, Section 13

Lily senses that the Ramsays have reached the lighthouse and suddenly feels exhausted. Carmichael looms up beside her and watches the lighthouse. She is aware that without speech both have shared the experience fully. She turns to her unfinished painting which, she acknowledges, is probably destined for someone's attic, and she notices that the triangular shadow has disappeared from the steps. Even as she realises this, she finally understands what must be done to complete the picture. She adds a line in the centre and lays down her brush in extreme fatigue, confident that at last her vision has been achieved.

The Ramsays' journey and Lily's internal quest are accomplished at the same time, and in Lily's acknowledgement of her communion with Carmichael is the validation of her recognition that human emotions, however limited, have their own value. With this recognition comes the ability to finish the painting with a symbolic brush stroke connecting the two sides of the picture. The completion of the painting and the end of the journey to the lighthouse happen simultaneously, bringing to a triumphant conclusion the narrative and symbolic levels of *To the Lighthouse*.

Part 3

Commentary

Point of view in *To the Lighthouse*

In all novels incidents, actions, thoughts and descriptions are related, or narrated, by an agent who is known as a *narrator*. The reader consequently sees the events of a novel to a greater or lesser degree through the eyes, or point of view, of the novel's narrator. It is obvious, therefore, that the narrator is an extremely significant element in considering a novel, because it is the narrator who decides what to show or tell us, and what emphasis is to be placed on an event or character, and it is the narrator's language that describes events and characters.

The novelist has, broadly speaking, three choices open to him when he comes to write a novel. The first of these is known as *omniscient narration* – the story is told by an omniscient narrator who has access to all the events as well as to the thoughts of his characters. The narrator can borrow the point of view of any character and observe events through that character's eyes. He can compress any part of the story and is free to make judgements upon actions and characters. By his emphasis of certain characters and events, by his choice of imagery and language, and through his direct criticism of events and characters, the character of the omniscient narrator is revealed to the reader. The *persona* of the omniscient narrator may dominate the novel, as in the case of *Vanity Fair* (1847–8), by W.M.Thackeray (1811–63), or *Middlemarch*, by George Eliot; but the omniscient narrator can equally make himself inconspicuous as Gustave Flaubert (1821–80) tried to do in *Madame Bovary* (1857). The omniscient narrator can minimise his presence in the novel by having his characters act and speak for themselves with very little overt comment. In this way the detached omniscient narrator forces his readers to make their own judgements about what is happening in the novel. The reader may even feel that he is seeing and hearing for himself, but it must never be forgotten that the reader's perception is still manipulated by the omniscient narrator's choice of incident, character and language. The existence of an omniscient narrator in a novel, obvious or otherwise, establishes an interpreter between the reader and the events of the novel, and clarifies for the reader what might otherwise be puzzling or annoying.

The novelist may choose a *first-person narrator* to tell his story. This is the technique used by Emily Brontë (1818–48) in *Wuthering Heights* (1847), and by Joseph Conrad (1857–1924) in *Heart of Darkness* (1902), and by Scott Fitzgerald (1896–1940) in *The Great Gatsby* (1925). If the novelist chooses such a narrator, he restricts himself to the observations of a single character. Such observations will be limited by that character's intelligence and by his moral and social perspectives. This first-person narrator interprets the story as he relates it, either overtly through criticism and commentary, or covertly through his choice of character and incident and through the language and imagery he may use. It is necessary, therefore, to be aware of clues to the character of the narrator which may be scattered through the novel, so that we can decide how reliable his information and judgements are. This first-person narrator may be an observer or an active participant in the events he narrates. The first-person narrator of Charles Dickens's (1812–70) *David Copperfield* (1849–50) – David himself – is clearly central to the events he describes; Nick Carraway, who recounts the *Gatsby* story, is only partially involved in the main events of this story; Lockwood, the narrator who begins the story in *Wuthering Heights*, is a complete spectator to events which have taken place long before he visits that farmhouse. This *narrator-agent* may use the first person ('I') or the third-person voice ('he', 'she', 'it', 'they' . . .). When the narrator-agent or the narrator-spectator is used in the third person, inexperienced readers may confuse them with the omniscient narrator, but the surest way of discriminating between these two modes of narration is to discover which character is the focus of the novel, and on the relationship between that central character and the events of the novel. When third-person narrator-agent mode is used, no event or occurrence will be narrated unless it has direct consequence for the main character. D.H.Lawrence's (1885–1930) *Sons and Lovers* (1913) is an example of such narration.

The third major mode of narration available to the novelist is through the direct transmission of the inner states of a character, persuading the reader that he is being directly confronted with the unedited mental experience of that character. William Faulkner's (1897–1962) *The Sound and the Fury* (1931) is such a novel. In many novels (*To the Lighthouse* is an example) the inner states of more than one character are dramatised, a method of narration known as *multiple inner points of view*. The mental processes of characters in these novels seem to be presented without any interference from the author. The external world is depicted through its reflection in the observing consciousnesses.

The effect of this narrative mode is to force the reader to construct the world of the novel for himself and to apply his own judgements to that world. While the omniscient narrator at one end of the scale of narration guides the reader carefully through the fictional world and the values by which that world is to be assessed, the multiple inner viewpoint novel provides no certain or reliable 'truths' and forces the reader to become the novelist's active partner in creating the novel's fictional world. Another effect of this narrative mode is to concentrate the reader's attention on how characters experience events rather than on what is experienced.

The story, or plot, of *To the Lighthouse* is extremely simple. In the first part, 'The Window', we are introduced to the main characters and the central issue: whether or not the planned expedition to the lighthouse will take place. The second part, 'Time Passes', covers a passage of ten years and reveals the deaths of several members of the Ramsay family. The final section, 'The Lighthouse', recounts how the expedition to the lighthouse, which was planned ten years earlier, is finally accomplished.

It is obvious from this bald description of the novel's plot that the reader's main interest in *To the Lighthouse* is not of the 'what happened next?' variety. The emphasis of this novel falls on how its events are experienced by those who participate, and the narration is carried out through the multiple point of view method, in which the reader has access to the mental processes of the various characters. This narrative mode provides a rich and complex perspective on the events and world of the novel. To take a simple example: Mrs Ramsay is variously presented as a tyrant, a heroine, uncompromising, pathetic, and lovable, depending on the angle of vision of the observing consciousness. Which impression is the right one? The answer is all, and none. Mrs Ramsay is, in the world of this novel, all of these.

Virginia Woolf's particular use of the multiple point of view technique in *To the Lighthouse* poses certain problems, however, for the reader. The uniformity of language and style in the novel makes it difficult to distinguish individual points of view. The language of the consciousness of the six-year-old James, for example, is remarkably similar in vocabulary and style to that of his eminent philosopher father. In this early, characteristic passage from the novel, the language and style of the two points of view are so similar as to be virtually indistinguishable:

> Such were the extremes of emotion that Mr Ramsay excited in his children's breasts by his mere presence; standing, as now, lean as a knife, narrow as the blade of one, grinning sarcastically, not only with the pleasure of disillusioning his son and casting ridicule upon his wife, who was ten thousand times better in every way than he was (James thought), but also with some secret conceit at his own

accuracy of judgement. What he said was true. It was always true. He was incapable of untruth; never tampered with a fact; never altered a disagreeable word to suit the pleasure or convenience of any mortal being, least of all his own children, who, sprung from his loins, should be aware from childhood that life is difficult; facts uncompromising; and the passage to that fabled land where our brightest hopes are extinguished, our frail barks founder in darkness (here Mr Ramsay would straighten his back and narrow his little blue eyes upon the horizon), one that needs, above all, courage, truth, and the power to endure (pp.9–10).

In this passage three consciousnesses or voices are at work; the omniscient narrator, young James and Mr Ramsay. We can discriminate one voice from another by the content of their thought and through the 'stage directions' of the omniscient narrator: but the style and language of the three is remarkably similar. This passage also demonstrates another difficulty in distinguishing the location of the point of view. The voices alternate so quickly that the unsophisticated reader may find himself baffled by the contradictory voices he hears.

The reader has several means of distinguishing the voices. The most obvious way to identify a voice is through the attribution of 'he said', 'she felt', and so on. Sometimes the content will indicate the source, as in this example of James's hostility towards his father and Ramsay's attitude towards the truth. Sometimes Mrs Woolf uses phrases or images which, through repetition, become associated with the consciousness of a particular character. Lily Briscoe's perception of Ramsay's intellect and its associations with the kitchen table, and Ramsay's image of human knowledge as an alphabet, are examples of such a use of imagery. Mrs Ramsay's frequent use of the phrase 'after all' represents a characteristically-repeated phrase.

In addition to the difficulties of distinguishing one point of view from another, an additional problem is raised in the discrimination of these points of view from the voice of the omniscient narrator, which is frequently intermingled with the other voices. The material presented by the omniscient narrator can often be identified by its indefiniteness in time and space, its tendency to generalise about people and life, and its extended perspective:

Never did anybody look so sad. Bitter and black, half-way down, in the darkness, in the shaft which ran from the sunlight to the depths, perhaps a tear formed; a tear fell; the waters swayed this way and that, received it, and were at rest. Never did anybody look so sad (p.31).

In addition to such material, the omniscient narrator's voice presents 'stage directions' such as 'he said', 'she thought', and so on. There are also certain characteristics both of style and tone which identify the omniscient narrator in *To the Lighthouse*. The reader will notice in the observation of the omniscient narrator a tone of hesitancy, of diffidence, which may lead him to question the omniscience of the narrator. In the passage just quoted, notice the repetition of the vague 'anybody' and the use of the hesitant 'perhaps'. This quality of doubt and uncertainty is unusual in the conventional omniscient narrator and gives the novel a characteristic quality which has been noted by many of its critics.

The three parts of the novel are dominated by separate voices which provide a certain tone and attitude to those parts. The first part, 'The Window', is largely presented through the consciousness of Mrs Ramsay as she sits by the window knitting, and later as she presides over the dinner party. The middle section of the novel, 'Time Passes', depends upon the voice of the omniscient narrator. The third and final section, 'The Lighthouse', is presented largely through the alternate consciousnesses of Lily and those on board the boat.

Characters in the novel

One effect of Virginia Woolf's choice of this multiple point of view narrative mode is immediately obvious when we examine the characters and characterisation of *To the Lighthouse*. Not only are these characters observed in action, or reflected in the consciousness of themselves and others, but their very perspective on external reality serves to define them. We cannot, for example, speak with confidence of Mrs Ramsay's goodness without acknowledging the reservations imposed by herself and the other characters upon that goodness; as well as taking into account the characteristic quality of Mrs Ramsay's view of the world. It is impossible, therefore, to make any clear-cut distinction between the characters in this novel and its narrative mode. Virginia Woolf's method of creating the characters in *To the Lighthouse* is, in a sense, a cumulative one. Our knowledge of the characters depends on the accumulated impressions of them we receive, both from their own reflections and observations and from the responses they elicit from the other characters. The reader is obliged to re-create for himself the characters of this novel.

Mr and Mrs Ramsay

The opening section of the novel gives us a clear impression of Mr and Mrs Ramsay. The two, as they are presented here, provide a study in contrasts; Mrs Ramsay is portrayed in images of softness and fertility –

the fountain, the flowering fruit tree – while Mr Ramsay is symbolised by the arid scimitar, the beak of brass. The husband-wife, male-female polarity of this opening section is a theme developed through the novel, and is reflected in the contrasting qualities of intellect possessed by both. Mrs Ramsay is portrayed as possessing instinctive, intuitive intelligence, while her husband's intellect is of the rational and orderly variety symbolised by his perception of human knowledge as a series of letters of the alphabet.

To over-emphasise the symmetry of these characteristics is, however, to do an injustice to the complexity and suggestiveness of the novel's characterisation. These symbolic intimations of character are part of a larger scheme of characterisation which provides a psychologically realistic series of portraits. A fine example of the powerful juxtaposition of symbolic and realistic portraiture can be found in the description of Mrs Ramsay as she sits with her husband after the dinner party. There is psychological realism in the description of her puzzling over her husband's desire for fame, and in the description of a mind drifting through association rather than logic from one idea to another. A short passage of heightened prose describes the hypnotic effect of the remembered line of poetry upon Mrs Ramsay, but the passage is firmly anchored in the external world by the description of Mrs Ramsay knitting, then stretching for a book on the table beside her:

> It didn't matter, any of it, she thought. A great man, a great book, fame – who could tell? She knew nothing about it. But it was his way with him, his truthfulness – for instance at dinner she had been thinking quite instinctively, If only he would speak! She had complete trust in him. And dismissing all this, as one passes in diving now a weed, now a straw, now a bubble, she felt again, sinking deeper, as she had felt in the hall when the others were talking, There is something I want – something I have come to get, and she fell deeper and deeper without knowing quite what it was, with her eyes closed. And she waited a little, knitting, wondering, and slowly those words they had said at dinner, 'the China rose is all abloom and buzzing with the honey bee', began washing from side to side of her mind rhythmically, and as they washed, words, like little shaded lights, one red, one blue, one yellow, lit up in the dark of her mind, and seemed leaving their perches up there to fly across and across, or to cry out and to be echoed; so she turned and felt on the table beside her for a book (p.109).

Because Mrs Ramsay's is the dominating point of view in the early sections of the novel, the reader may easily be persuaded to take her side. She appears to represent femininity, maternity and sympathy, and we feel some aversion from the uncompromisingly severe truth-fulness of Ramsay and Charles Tansley. Our sympathy is increased when we look through her eyes at her reflection in the mirror and see a fading beauty who is a model of unselfishness:

> When she looked in the glass and saw her hair grey, her cheek sunk, at fifty, she thought, possibly she might have managed things better – her husband; money; his books. But for her own part she would never for a single second regret her decision, evade difficulties, or slur over duties (pp.11–12).

This early limited version of her character and that of her husband is soon modified by her complex reflections about Charles Tansley, who arouses in her a mixture of maternal desire to please and protect and an equally strong feeling of repugnance based on his awkwardness. Her attitude towards the young student reveals social condescension and snobbery. When her husband corrects her forecast of the weather, she responds with strong anger to what she feels is a blindness to the feelings of others, and a sense of martyrdom and moral superiority. She dwells on their financial insecurity and her suspicion that his most recent book is not as successful as earlier ones. Another guest, Mr Carmichael, makes her feel uncomfortable because he makes no demands on her; her characteristic response is to feel pity for him. Yet she is aware of the ambiguity of her emotional response, however much she may try to evade personal responsibility:

> For her own self-satisfaction was it that she wished so instinctively to help, to give, that people might say of her, 'O Mrs Ramsay! dear Mrs Ramsay . . . Mrs Ramsay, of course!' and need her and send for her and admire her? Was it not secretly this that she wanted, and therefore when Mr Carmichael shrank away from her, as he did at this moment, making off to some corner where he did acrostics endlessly, she did not feel merely snubbed back in her instinct, but made aware of the pettiness of some part of her, and of human relations, how flawed they are, how despicable, how self-seeking at their best (pp.42–3).

She wishes to keep her youngest son and daughter in a state of perpetual childhood, and she admits to herself that she prefers 'boobies' to intelligent young men, for she can control children and boobies. This manipulative element in her character is alien to her perception of herself, and she is puzzled that Minta's mother should have accused her of alienating her daughter's affections. Mrs Ramsay defends herself from this accusation by direct reference to her appearance, to her fading beauty and to the shabbiness of her clothes, all of which are made to reflect her internal self-sacrifice as a kind of theatrical costume signifying goodness and thereby absolving her of hostile criticism.

Mrs Ramsay instinctively identifies herself with Lily the artist and with Carmichael the poet. Like them, she is a creator but her medium is human beings and her form, human relationships. The novel makes it clear that she is only partially successful in her art; the radiance of her dinner party may draw people together momentarily, but it is inevitably destroyed by time. Paul and Minta may have their courtship of intense happiness under her guidance, but time destroys their marriage. Mrs Ramsay's attempts to shield her children from the forces of mutability are defeated and she too is destroyed by her familiar antagonist, death.

The complexity of Mrs Ramsay's character is revealed through her consciousness of reality and the language and images she uses to describe it. It is created also through her reflection in the eyes of the other characters. The three male guests, Tansley, Bankes and Carmichael show varying responses to her. Carmichael is emotionally self-sufficient and is aware of the degree of manipulation involved in Mrs Ramsay's self-sacrifice. Bankes, Ramsay's longtime friend and colleague, responds to her mystery and beauty, but is also partially conscious of her destructive powers. Tansley also responds to her beauty, but is even more attracted by her pity for him. The young couple, Paul and Minta, are completely under her spell and obey her wish that they should marry. The Ramsay children respond with love and with varying degrees of admiration, ranging from James who adores her unquestioningly, to Jasper who reflects that 'being his mother she lived away in another division of the world' (p.77).

Lily Briscoe's perception of and response to Mrs Ramsay is more complex than any of the other characters. She is fully aware of her friend's ability to dominate through love and pity, but she also recognises her worth. Of all the characters in the novel, Lily is the one who most fully grasps the ambiguities of her hostess's character and comes to love the whole Mrs Ramsay. It is Lily who has the final vision of Mrs Ramsay, and it is Lily who makes that vision permanent through her art.

Mr Ramsay is, in many respects, the direct antithesis of his wife. He loves her very deeply, but can still be infuriated by her disrespect for factual truth. His worship of truth matters more to him than the feelings of his friends and family. His intellectual integrity gives him a quality of aloofness, but this is deceptive for he loves and needs his family more than his seemingly emotional but inwardly withdrawn wife. Unlike Mrs Ramsay, Mr Ramsay gives little thought to his effect on others; he stalks around the garden reciting poetry aloud, contemptuous of the responses of his family and guests. He makes overt demands on the sympathies and emotions of those around him. These traits are quite different from his wife's acute self-consciousness and her covert manipulation of others.

Like the character of Mrs Ramsay, Mr Ramsay's is portrayed through his own consciousness and through the eyes of those who see him. An apparently contradictory web of images surrounds him: he is hard and arid like a scimitar, cruel as a beak of brass that gorges upon his wife's energy and fertility. Yet he is also an intrepid explorer, the sailor who travels where lesser mortals do not dare. He is a loving, protective paterfamilias who responds with warmth to the sight of a mother hen and her chickens, and who can be overwhelmed by admiration for his wife. The other characters, especially Bankes and Lily, flesh out the details of his portrait. Bankes remembers Ramsay as a young batchelor and, in accordance with Bankes's own emotional aridity, regrets the domestic and emotional aspects of Ramsay's life which, he feels, have weakened his potential and destroyed their friendship. Yet Bankes envies his friend and sees him in a powerful image that combines elements of Ramsay's intellectual integrity and domestic affection as the father with the child on his shoulder, looking 'at a picture of Vesuvius in eruption' (p.26). Lily is, once more, the most astute and balanced of the observers, noticing his single-minded fidelity to the truth as well as his egotistical pursuit of sympathy and admiration, while acknowledging his tenderness and courage.

In Virginia Woolf's portrayal of Mrs Ramsay following the dinner party we noted a balance between symbolism and realism in the very language and style of the novel. This equilibrium is apparent also in the depiction of the Ramsays as a couple. Their portrait is drawn in a manner which makes them credible in terms of psychological realism but they exist also as powerful, generalised symbols. At one point, Lily has a glimpse of them in their symbolic guise as an image of marriage:

That is what Mrs Ramsay tried to tell me the other night, she thought. For she was wearing a green shawl, and they were standing close together watching Prue and Jasper throwing catches. And suddenly the meaning which, for no reason at all, as perhaps they are stepping out of the Tube or ringing a doorbell, descends on people, making them symbolical, making them representative, came upon them, and made them in the dusk standing, looking, the symbols of marriage, husband and wife. Then, after an instant, the symbolical outline which transcended the real figures sank down again, and they became, as they met them, Mr and Mrs Ramsay watching the children throwing catches . . . still, for one moment, there was a sense of things having been blown apart, of space, of irresponsibility as the ball soared high, and they followed it and lost it and saw the one star and the draped branches (p.69).

There is a generalised quality about many of the images associated with the Ramsays so that, without losing their credibility as individuals and particularised characters, they exist also as types of husband and wife, man and woman, reason and intuition, science and art.

Lily Briscoe

Lily Briscoe is first seen through the eyes of Mrs Ramsay, whose values severely slant the portrait:

> But the sight of the girl standing on the edge of the lawn painting reminded her; she was supposed to be keeping her head as much in the same position as possible for Lily's picture. Lily's picture! Mrs Ramsay smiled. With her little Chinese eyes and her puckered-up face she would never marry; one could not take her painting very seriously; but she was an independent little creature, Mrs Ramsay liked her for it, and so remembering her promise, she bent her head (p.21).

This first glimpse shows Lily standing apart from the other characters, 'on the edge of the lawn painting', and this relationship to the others is significant, for Lily is to be the onlooker and artist in the novel, complementing the characters of Mr and Mrs Ramsay and rounding out the complex presentation of truth which is at the heart of it.

As well as being an indispensable and objective observer of the Ramsays and the other inhabitants of the house, Lily exists as a force in her own right, refusing to bow to Mrs Ramsay's covert pressure to marry and refusing also to succumb to the austere attractions of emotional isolation represented by such characters as Carmichael and Bankes. Lily's painting and its completion are a literal and symbolic expression of her ability to balance conflicting pressure in life. Parallel to the narrative progression of the novel is Lily's spiritual pilgrimage from the position of outsider to the one who stands at the centre of a vision which she alone translates into the indestructible form of art.

The other guests

The other guests display in their portrayal a range of particularisation, from Tansley who is presented in some detail, to Carmichael the poet who seems to hover at the edges of the novel as a presence rather than a fully-realised individual.

Charles Tansley is an unsympathetic character, a young academic who has struggled against his poverty-stricken background and is bitterly conscious of his social inadequacy when confronted by the upper middle-class world inhabited by the Ramsays and their other guests. His bitterness is more profound than his sense of social inadequacy because, as Lily remembers, even when he does achieve a measure of success, his attitudes remain harsh and unloving:

> She had gone one day into a Hall and heard him speaking during the war. He was denouncing something: he was condemning somebody. He was preaching brotherly love (p.181).

William Bankes provides quite a different perspective on the Ramsays. He can remember Ramsay before his marriage, and he has the experience and confidence to make a professional judgement on his friend. Bankes's austere emotional life, which he has deliberately chosen, provides a contrast to the emotional perspectives of the three central characters, Mr and Mrs Ramsay and Lily.

Carmichael, the elderly poet and opium addict, exists in the first section of the novel through the eyes of the other characters. We are informed by the omniscient narrator, and later by Lily, that the war has somehow stimulated his poetry and he has become famous. As an artist, he is a companion figure to Lily and stands with her on the edge of the lawn as she completes her painting.

Although *Paul and Minta* are given a number of individual characteristics, their existence in the novel is more symbolic than realistic. They represent youthful passion in the eyes of Lily and Mrs Ramsay, and the radiance of this passion is an important element in the fulfilment achieved by Mrs Ramsay at the dinner party. Their marriage is, however, a failure, so they provide yet another perspective on the successful Ramsay relationship.

Mrs McNab and the even shadowier figure of *Mrs Bast*, who come to put the house in order following the ten-year absence of the Ramsays, exist primarily as symbols of human effort against the ruthless forces of cosmic disaster. Mrs McNab, in particular, seems to be the embodiment of womankind at its most basic, at one remove from the fertility of nature. She seems indifferent to the world, and despite occasional flashes of humour, her lack of intelligence, her insensitivity to a life other than the warmth of the local public house and its gossip, make her a direct contrast to the Ramsays. Yet it is she who physically rescues the house from the ravages of the elements.

The children

Early in the novel, Mr Bankes thinks of the eight Ramsay children in the following terms:

> As for being sure which was which, or in what order they came, that was beyond him. He called them privately after the Kings and

Queens of England; Cam the Wicked, James the Ruthless, Andrew the Just, Prue the Fair – for Prue would have beauty, he thought, how could she help it? – and Andrew brains (pp.25–6).

Mr Bankes's impression is shared by many readers of *To the Lighthouse* because the characters of the children are drawn, for the most part, in broad, bold outline. Andrew, the eldest boy, shows great promise, but this promise is destroyed by his death. Prue, the eldest girl, is largely characterised by her budding beauty, also destroyed by untimely death. Jasper shoots at the rooks against his mother's wishes. Nancy is a member of the expedition to the beach. She is interested in the rock pools and deeply disturbed by Paul and Minta's kiss. Rose, who chooses the jewellery for her mother and arranges the centrepiece of fruit for the dinner party, is deeply attached to her mother, showing a devotion that Mrs Ramsay guiltily acknowledges she cannot return.

The two youngest children, Cam and James, are the most clearly delineated. They are also the two who accompany Mr Ramsay to the lighthouse, and their journey provides a symbolic parallel to their spiritual growth under the influence of both parents. In the course of the sea voyage, both come to recognise, in quite different ways, that neither of the parents has a monopoly on truth or goodness, and that life, symbolised by the lighthouse, is a complex and frequently contradictory process.

Symbolism

Much of the significance of *To the Lighthouse* is created by its symbolic structure, which pushes the immediate reference of the story and the individual characters on to a more general level, where they represent the common human experience of the encounter against time, death and the cosmic forces that forever threaten to destroy man.

So closely is the symbolic material interwoven with the psychologically realistic details of the novel that the separation of symbolic elements from the rest of the novel and from each other does *To the Lighthouse* an injustice.

When literary critics use the word 'symbolism', what do they mean? In *Theory of Literature*, Wellek and Warren suggest that in literary criticism the usage of 'symbolism' be confined to discussion of '. . . an object which refers to another object but which demands attention also in its own right'.[1] This description of symbolism indicates the dual nature of the symbol in literature, existing on the level of representa-

[1]Rene Wellek and Austin Warren, *Theory of Literature*, new revised edition, Harcourt, Brace & World, New York, 1962, p.189.

tional realism (demanding attention in its own right) as well as pointing towards another object or area of experience. Thus, an object like the lighthouse in *To the Lighthouse* exists on one level as a lighthouse in the fictional world of the novel, while also directing the reader towards another kind of truth. In a letter to her friend, the artist and critic Roger Fry, Virginia Woolf seems to have agreed with such an understanding of symbolism:

> I meant *nothing* by *The Lighthouse*. One has to have a central line down the middle of the book to hold the design together. I saw that all sorts of feelings would accrue to this, but I refused to think them out, and trusted that people would make it the deposit for their own emotions – which they have done, one thinking it means one thing another another. I can't manage Symbolism except in this vague, generalised way. Whether it's right or wrong I don't know; but directly I'm told what a thing means, it becomes hateful to me.[2]

Virtually every detail of the world created in *To the Lighthouse* can be seen to contain some symbolic suggestion and it would be impossible to trace and assess the development of each individual symbol. What follows is an attempt to describe, in the widest sense, certain major groups of associated symbols which, intertwined with each other and with the diverse elements of the novel, create what we may describe as the 'meaning' of the novel.

The sea

The sea is a powerful element in the setting of *To the Lighthouse*. The Ramsays' summer house is situated on an island which faces the smaller island on which the lighthouse stands.

The sea pervades the lives of the Ramsays and their guests. The house is full of bric-a-brac from sea and beach which the children have collected, so that the sea is physically present even in the house. The sound of the waves is a constant background to the sounds of house and garden. This sound raises ambivalent feelings in Mrs Ramsay, representing to her both the reassuring permanence of natural forces and their potential to destroy:

> . . . the monotonous fall of the waves on the beach, which for the most part beat a measured and soothing tattoo to her thoughts and seemed consolingly to repeat over and over again as she sat with the children the words of some old cradle song, murmured by nature, 'I am guarding you – I am your support', but at other times suddenly and unexpectedly, especially when her mind raised itself slightly

[2] *A Change of Perspective: the Letters of Virginia Woolf 1923–1928*, p.385.

from the task actually in hand, had no such kindly meaning, but like a ghostly roll of drums remorselessly beat the measure of life, made one think of the destruction of the island and its engulfment in the sea, and warned her whose day had slipped past in one quick doing after another that it was all ephemeral as a rainbow – this sound which had been obscured and concealed under the other sounds suddenly thundered hollow in her ears and made her look up with an impulse of terror (p.20).

Mr Ramsay, frequently depicted by the image of the sailor-explorer, faces the infinity of the sea, which suggests to him the vast expanse of human knowledge yet to be explored, at once terrifying and challenging:

He reached the edge of the lawn and looked out on the bay beneath.

It was his fate, his peculiarity, whether he wished it or not, to come out thus on a spit of land which the sea is slowly eating away, and there to stand, like a desolate sea-bird, alone. It was his power, his gift, suddenly to shed all superfluities, to shrink and diminish so that he looked barer and felt sparer, even physically, yet lost none of his intensity of mind, and so to stand on his little ledge facing the dark of human ignorance, how we know nothing and the sea eats away the ground we stand on – that was his fate, his gift (p.44).

The seascape which can be seen from the garden becomes a focus for the feelings of Mr and Mrs Ramsay, bringing them together in spite of their differences:

. . . the whole bay spread before them and Mrs Ramsay could not help exclaiming, 'Oh how beautiful!' For the great plateful of blue water was before her; the hoary Lighthouse, distant, austere, in the midst; and on the right, as far as the eye could see, fading and falling, in soft low pleats, the green sand dunes with the wild flowing grasses on them, which always seemed to be running away into some moon country, uninhabited of men.

That was the view, she said, stopping, growing greyer-eyed, that her husband loved (p.17).

While it is the benevolent aspect of the sea that is most in evidence in 'The Window', in 'Time Passes' its destructive aspect is dramatised. We learn of shipwrecks and storms, and the sea assumes a malevolent character:

There was the silent apparition of an ashen-coloured ship for instance, come, gone; there was a purplish stain upon the bland surface of the sea as if something had boiled and bled, invisibly, beneath. This intrusion into a scene calculated to stir the most sublime reflections and lead to the most comfortable conclusions stayed their pacing. It was difficult blandly to overlook them, to abolish their significance in the landscape; to continue, as one walked by the sea, to marvel how beauty outside mirrored beauty within (pp.124–5).

In the final part, 'The Lighthouse', both aspects are reconciled in the perceptions of the various characters and this reconciliation is an aspect of the internal voyage undergone by the main characters. Mr Ramsay lives up to the promise of his image as the brave sailor, leading his little band across the dangerous sea to safety. Cam comes to terms with the past and her fear of death through the security her father's presence confers. For Lily, as she paints, the sea becomes part of a whole which can be encompassed by her art:

So much depends then, thought Lily Briscoe, looking at the sea which had scarcely a stain on it, which was so soft that the sails and the clouds seemed set in its blue, so much depends, she thought, upon distance: whether people are near us or far from us; for her feeling for Mr Ramsay changed as he sailed further and further across the bay. It seemed to be elongated, stretched out; he seemed to become more and more remote. He and his children seemed to be swallowed up in that blue, that distance . . . She seemed to be standing up to the lips in some substance, to move and float and sink in it, yes, for these waters were unfathomably deep. Into them had spilled so many lives. The Ramsays'; the children's; and all sorts of waifs and strays of things besides. A washerwoman with her basket; a rook; a red-hot poker; the purples and grey-greens of flowers: some common feeling which held the whole together (pp.176–7).

The land

In contrast with the mysterious cosmic forces that are symbolised by the sea, the land – the house on the island, the garden, the sand dunes – represents a precarious human stronghold. The house, Mrs Ramsay's domain, is a haven of tranquillity for family and guests, but its invulnerability is an illusion. In the early part of the novel, we learn that the children bring their sea treasures into the house, and after the death of Mrs Ramsay, the house falls prey to the destructive forces in nature. The garden also, time-honoured symbol of man's ability to tame nature, is quickly overpowered by the elements in man's relatively brief absence. House and garden are both recovered from these forces through human determination and effort, but, in keeping

with the general theme of the novel, neither can ever be completely
restored to its earlier state:

Ah, said Mrs Bast, they'd find it changed. She leant out of the
window. She watched her son George scything the grass. They might
well ask, what had been done to it? seeing how old Kennedy was
supposed to have charge of it, and then his leg got so bad he fell from
the cart; and perhaps then no one for a year, or the better part of
one; and then Davie Macdonald, and seeds might be sent, but who
should say if they were ever planted? They'd find it changed
(p.131).

Mr Ramsay associates himself with the sand dunes, that mysterious
territory between sea and land. 'That was the country he liked best,
over there; those sandhills dwindling away into darkness' (p.66).
When Mr Bankes thinks of his friendship with Ramsay, he looks towards the sand dunes: 'But in this dumb colloquy with the sand dunes
he maintained that his affection for Ramsay had in no way diminished'
(p.24). The climax of Bankes's meditation is associated with the sand
dunes:

. . . there like the body of a young man laid up in peat for a
century, with the red fresh on his lips, was his friendship, in its
acuteness and reality laid up across the bay among the sandhills
(p.24).

The lighthouse

The lighthouse, as the title of the novel suggests, and as Virginia
Woolf acknowledged in her letter to Roger Fry[3], is the central symbol
of the novel. It is associated with the many images of light and darkness that occur in the novel, as well as with the sea and land imagery.
Mrs Ramsay, as she bargains with death and change, attempts to create
and preserve the light. Ramsay is concerned with the dark reaches of
human ignorance. When Carmichael extinguishes his lamp at the
beginning of 'Time Passes', it is the signal for the invasion of the house
by the sinister forces of nature. Lily's painting attempts to capture this
quality of life, of light:

But the picture was not of them, she said. Or, not in his sense.
There were other senses, too, in which one might reverence them.
By a shadow here and a light there, for instance. Her tribute took
that form, if, as she vaguely supposed, a picture must be a tribute.
A mother and child might be reduced to a shadow without ir-
reverence. A light here required a shadow there (p.52).

[3]ibid.

The atmosphere and achievement of Mrs Ramsay's dinner party are expressed also in the imagery of light and darkness. Paul Rayley, entering the house when he returns from the beach with Minta, notices especially the lights. Mrs Ramsay is surrounded by a 'golden haze', and the lights on the table separate the guests from the darkness of the outside world:

> Now all the candles were lit, and the faces on both sides of the table were brought nearer by the candle light, and composed, as they had not been in the twilight, into a party round a table, for the night was now shut off by panes of glass, which, far from giving any accurate view of the outside world, rippled it so strangely that here, inside the room, seemed to be order and dry land; there, outside, a reflection in which things wavered and vanished, waterily (pp.90–1).

The alternating light and darkness represented in this imagery is amplified by the lighthouse itself, sending its beam across the sea to the house and land. Mrs Ramsay particularly identifies with the light that comes from the lighthouse: 'she looked at the steady light, the pitiless, the remorseless, which was so much her, yet so little her, which had her at its beck and call (she woke in the night and saw it bent across their bed, stroking the floor) . . .' (p.62). Her thoughts reach a climax as she faces the power of the lighthouse over sea and darkness:

> . . . but for all that she thought, watching it with fascination, hypnotised, as if it were stroking with its silver fingers some sealed vessel in her brain whose bursting would flood her with delight, she had known happiness, exquisite happiness, intense happiness, and it silvered the rough waves a little more brightly, as daylight faded, and the blue went out of the sea and it rolled in waves of pure lemon which curved and swelled and broke upon the beach and the ecstasy burst in her eyes and waves of pure delight raced over the floor of her mind and she felt, It is enough! It is enough! (pp.62–3).

In the 'Time Passes' section, the lighthouse, cut off from human associations, becomes an ambivalent observer of the chaos which descends upon the house:

> When darkness fell, the stroke of the Lighthouse, which had laid itself with such authority upon the carpet in the darkness, tracing its pattern, came now in the softer light of spring mixed with moonlight gliding gently as if it laid it caress and lingered stealthily and looked and came lovingly again. But in the very lull of this loving caress, as the long stroke leant upon the bed, the rock was rent asunder; another fold of the shawl loosened; there it hung, and swayed (pp.123–4).

Just as its light is powerless to stay the destruction of house and garden, so too it fails to save the local fishermen who are drowned nearby.

The final section of the novel, 'The Lighthouse', uses the lighthouse as a central focus for the narrative and symbolic structure of the novel. On the narrative level, Ramsay and his two children finally make the journey to the lighthouse, and on the symbolic level these three characters, and Lily Briscoe, accomplish an internal journey until they can accept that truth is frequently contradictory. The dual image of the lighthouse as it is seen by James represents this synthesis very powerfully:

> James looked at the Lighthouse. He could see the white-washed rocks; the tower, stark and straight; he could see that it was barred with black and white; he could see windows in it; he could even see washing spread on the rocks to dry. So that was the Lighthouse, was it? No, the other was also the Lighthouse. For nothing was simply one thing. The other was the Lighthouse too. It was sometimes hardly to be seen across the bay. In the evening one looked up and saw the eye opening and shutting and the light seemed to reach them in that airy sunny garden where they sat (p.172).

Mr Ramsay's spiritual renewal is signalled by the last glimpse we have of him, springing 'lightly like a young man', towards the lighthouse (p.191). For Lily, the final stage of her inward journey occurs at the moment of Ramsay's landing, when the lighthouse has become almost invisible (p.191). The final line of her painting, drawing all together, represents the lighthouse, 'a line there, in the centre' (p.192).

Part 4

Hints for study

Is *To the Lighthouse* a novel?

To the Lighthouse struck the majority of its first readers as a startling and original experiment in extending the range of the novel. Whether or not it is a successful novel, however, is a question that continues to perplex critics. Every new work of art forces us to re-examine our definitions of art, and, in assessing Virginia Woolf's achievement in *To the Lighthouse*, we must reconsider fundamental assumptions about the novel form itself.

Virginia Woolf's diary

Two entries in Virginia Woolf's diary are frequently quoted as evidence of her own perception that *To the Lighthouse* was not, properly speaking, a novel:

> (But while I try to write, I am making up *To the Lighthouse* – the sea is to be heard all through it. I have an idea that I will invent a new name for my books to supplant 'novel'. A new —— by Virginia Woolf. But what? Elegy?)[1]

> Well Leonard has read *To the Lighthouse* and says it is much my best book and it is a 'masterpiece'. He said this without my asking . . . He calls it entirely new – 'a psychological poem' is his name for it.[2]

What is a novel?

Most analyses of the novel identify four distinguishing elements: plot, character, setting, and the point(s) of view of the narrator(s). Through these devices the novelist creates a fictional world which stands at a certain angle to that world of everyday experience which we call 'reality'. Wellek and Warren argue:

> We are content to call a novelist great when his world, though not patterned or scaled like our own, is comprehensive of all the elements which we find necessary to catholic scope or, though narrow in

[1]*A Writer's Diary*, p.80.
[2]ibid., p.103.

scope, selects for inclusion the deep and central, and when the scale or hierarchy of elements seems to us such as a mature man can entertain.[3]

Others, of whom censors are an extreme example, have a more limited understanding of the novel's relationship to the real world.

To the Lighthouse can be criticised on all these counts – plot, character, setting, narrative style and its relationship to reality.

Plot in *To the Lighthouse*

Is *To the Lighthouse* a novel without a plot?

'*To the Lighthouse* is not a novel because it lacks a plot.' Discuss.

The novel traditionally directs our attention to a sequence of events and their outcome in time. We call this feature of the novel its plot, and in the conventional novels of the nineteenth century plot was the central organisational structure in the novel.

Plot as a sequence of events taking place in clock time exists in *To the Lighthouse* but it is not the sole organisational structure. Plot hinges on an answer to the question: will the Ramsays visit the lighthouse? The incidents depicted by Virginia Woolf are selected to have some bearing on the answer, but what makes this novel so innovative is the subservience of plot to another kind of development based on symbols and usually associated with poetry. Two equal levels of reality are portrayed in *To the Lighthouse*: the surface level of external action and appearance governed by clock time, and the inner level of mental reflection and personality expressed through symbol rather than plot. Mrs Ramsay conveys this dual reality:

. . . one after another, she, Lily, Augustus Carmichael, must feel, our apparitions, the things you know us by, are simply childish. Beneath it is all dark, it is all spreading, it is unfathomably deep; but now and again we rise to the surface and that is what you see us by (p.60).

When the novelist shifts our attention from the depiction of external reality to internal experience, from objectivity to subjectivity, some substitute for plot must be found to bring the novel together and sustain the reader's interest. Questions about the Ramsays' possible visit to the lighthouse do not stimulate of themselves sufficient interest to maintain the reader's attention and so Virginia Woolf provides parallel development in a series of interlocking symbols whose deepening meanings give momentum to the depiction of internal truths.

[3] *Theory of Literature*, p.214.

It must be emphasised that these parallel structures of plot and symbol do not compete in *To the Lighthouse* but coincide almost exactly. If we examine four of the central episodes of the plot – the opening section which introduces Mr and Mrs Ramsay, the dinner party, the landing at the lighthouse, and the completion of the portrait – it is clear that all these external incidents have an equally strong significance at the symbolical level. Similarly, the most obviously symbolic section of the novel, 'Time Passes', never strays far from the depiction of realistic detail.

To answer any question about the nature or role of plot in *To the Lighthouse*, you must come to your own decision about what constitutes plot in the novel and what are the limitations of development through symbol in the novel.

Suggested reading

To the Lighthouse: Part 1, Section 1; 'Time Passes'; Part 3, Sections 12 and 13.
Virginia Woolf's *Collected Essays:* 'Impassioned Prose'; *'Aurora Leigh'*

Characterisation

'(Virginia Woolf) could seldom so portray a character that it was remembered afterwards on its own account . . .' (E.M. Forster). Discuss.
The poetic qualities of *To the Lighthouse* prevent Virginia Woolf from presenting characters fully in the novel. Comment.

In the conventional nineteenth-century novel, characters were depicted through their actions and words, through the judgements of other characters and through the overt and covert judgements of the narrator. These techniques all imply a belief that character is knowable, that the essence of personality can be learned from external appearance and behaviour. Virginia Woolf did not share this view of human nature[4] and the central characters in *To the Lighthouse* frequently comment on the nature of character and on the impossibility of every fully knowing or depicting character.

More than the overt commentary on human nature, the very form of *To the Lighthouse* provides a radically new commentary on the meaning of human nature. In the world of this novel, where even external reality is ambiguous, the reality of character is shadowy and frequently contradictory. Characters in *To the Lighthouse* are

[4]See Virginia Woolf, 'Mr Bennett and Mrs Brown', *Collected Essays I*, ed. Leonard Woolf, Chatto & Windus, London, 1967, pp.319–37.

combinations of opposites: loving and reserved, selfish and generous, cold and passionate.

What techniques are responsible for the creation of these new kinds of character? The number of points of view in *To the Lighthouse* is responsible for much of the conditional quality we find in the characterisation. The reader's impressions of each character are cumulative, developing both from his perception of that character's actions and growth over the duration of the novel, and also from the many versions of a character presented by the different narrators. The reader is left finally to construct his own single, unified version of the novel's characters from the multiple glimpses which the novel affords. The opening section of *To the Lighthouse* provides a vivid example of how rich and complex this method of characterisation is. Here Mr and Mrs Ramsay, their son James and the unpleasant Mr Tansley are introduced to the reader through their words and actions as these are variously reflected in the viewpoints of the narrators.

This opening section of the novel also provides several typical examples of Virginia Woolf's use of symbol to create character. By their nature symbols do not directly represent the inner states of the characters, but point towards something which will suggest those states. The extensive use of symbol in *To the Lighthouse*, particularly in the creation of character, extends the boundaries of conventional characterisation in the novel by directing the reader's attention away from the details of external appearance and action towards a deeper, more complete grasp of inner character. Symbols blur the individual sharpness of the characters, making them more universal and more accessible – a useful consideration in assessing this novel, which relies so heavily on Virginia Woolf's private memories.

Symbols – objects taken from the level of external reality – are associated with characters and relationships, and through repetition in different contexts their meaning and suggestiveness deepen, increasing our understanding of those characters who are associated with the symbols. In *To the Lighthouse*, the development of symbols has partly replaced the unfolding of action (plot) as the central moving force in the novel, and, when a major symbol is closely associated with a character, its development both increases our understanding of the character and advances the novel's symbolic action.

The symbol of the scimitar and beak of brass which the jealous James associates with his father in the opening section recurs frequently in the novel, its significance finally reaching a climax in the last part of the novel when James is reconciled to his father. The harshness and potential destructiveness signified by these two images are partially true in the light of Ramsay's ruthlessness; they accurately reflect James's hostility towards his father and specifically, towards his father's masculinity. James's final reconciliation with him is extended through the power of the symbols' suggestiveness to include acceptance of himself as a male, and final liberation from the destructive 'feminine' qualities of his mother. This example indicates symbolism's ability to replace conventional 'plot' as a satisfactory method of characterisation in the novel.

The coexistence of two levels of reality, external and internal, so much part of the meaning of this novel, springs from the very technique of *To the Lighthouse*. Many critics have commented upon the juxtaposition of sharp, naturalistic detail with passages of intensely figurative description, and Virginia Woolf's most typical characters combine both realities. Their external appearances are familiar to us – Mrs Ramsay's beauty, Lily's ugliness, Carmichael's opium-stained beard – but these are secondary to internal reality. External appearances provide the point of departure for highly figurative passages describing interior truths.

This method of portraying character is inseparable from the meaning of the novel. Characters possess a complex reality, existing both on the surface level of appearances and on an inner level of consciousness and subjectivity. At no point, however, does the reader forget the external character, for Virginia Woolf's techniques of multiple point of view, symbolism and style serve to present simultaneously the exterior and interior character.

Suggested readings from 'To the Lighthouse'

Commentary on personality
Part I, Section 9, p.51:
'How then, she had asked herself . . . the hives which were people.'
Part I, Section 11, p.60:
'Although she continued to knit . . . what you see us by.'
Part III, Section 5, pp.159–60:
'Who knows what we are? . . . Aren't we more expressive thus?'
Relationship between external and internal characterisation
Part I, Section 5, p.32:
'She clapped a deer-stalker's hat . . . to be like other people, insignificant.'
Part I, Section 7, pp.38–9:
'Mrs Ramsay, who had been sitting loosely . . . must be filled with life.'
Part III, Section 12, p.186:
'Mr Ramsay had almost done reading . . . the truth about things.'

Other reading

VIRGINIA WOOLF: *Collected Essays:* 'Mr Bennett and Mrs Brown'.
ERIC AUERBACH: *Mimesis: the representation of reality in Western literature*, trans. by Willard R. Trask, Princeton University Press, Princeton, 1946, pp.525–41, 546–53.

Use of symbols

Virginia Woolf substituted poetic structure for narrative structure in *To the Lighthouse*. Discuss.

'Holding on with one hand to poetry, she stretches and stretches to grasp things which are best gained by letting go of poetry' (E.M. Forster). Did Virginia Woolf succeed in writing a poetic novel with *To the Lighthouse*?

A major difference between *To the Lighthouse* and more conventional novels is the structural role played by symbol in Virginia Woolf's novel. Even its title is symbolic, referring at once to the literal journey undertaken by Mr Ramsay and his children and to several internal journeys taken by central characters. Any critical approach to this novel must take into account its symbolic dimension: character, setting, plot and the three-part structure of the novel all have symbolic as well as literal levels of meaning.

Characters as symbols

Lily and the Ramsays, central characters in the novel, possess symbolic significance, rarely emphasised in the novel because of Virginia Woolf's understanding that characters must be particularised individuals in order to hold the reader's attention and meet the most fundamental requirements of the novel genre. The main characters in *To the Lighthouse* possess the particular detail required by the novel, but exist also as symbols of truths larger than themselves. Lily's perception of the Ramsays (Part I, Section 13, p.69) as symbols of marriage is an overt signal to the reader that the characters have symbolical significance, but there are also many hidden signs of the symbolic meaning of characters, such as Lily's role as an artist, Carmichael's as a poet, and so on.

Lily's perception of the Ramsays as symbols of marriage provides a clue to Virginia Woolf's technique in making her characters symbolise truths larger than themselves. Lily begins by describing details of their appearance and moves from these to more generalised characteristics. This is the method Virginia Woolf herself uses to reveal the symbolic dimensions of her characters. In this way, her novel never completely departs from the novel's traditional description of external people and events while exploiting a larger symbolical meaning usually associated with poetry.

Setting as symbol

One of the traditional hallmarks of the novel is its creation of a world which, while not the real world of our everyday experience, has a clearly recognisable relation to that world. The setting of *To the Lighthouse* is a remote Scottish island where the Ramsay family and friends come for their summer holidays. There are numerous references to the island, the lighthouse which stands on a nearby island, the local town, the house and garden, and above all to the eternally present sea; but despite these concrete references (the novel is, of course, based on visits to Cornwall) it would be impossible for the reader to discover exact counterparts in the real world.

The timeless natural background for the events and characters of the novel enhances their symbolic qualities, and natural setting itself becomes a dynamic force in the 'Time Passes' section when the elements of climate, vegetative growth and the seasons show their hostility towards human order. These elements, recognisably part of the world of common human experience, are brought together in the world of the novel to suggest symbolically those forces of death, change and natural disaster against which the human spirit constantly struggles. This symbolic significance of setting is a cumulative process and therefore impossible to attribute to any one excerpt from the novel, but a brief examination of two related passages shows certain characteristics of Virginia Woolf's treatment of landscape as symbol in *To the Lighthouse*.

Passages for examination

Part I, Section 4, pp.23–4:
  'They came there regularly every evening . . . a sky which beholds an earth entirely at rest.'
Part II, Section 6, pp.124–5:
  'A shell exploded . . . the mirror was broken.'

The first passage describes the seascape as seen by Bankes and Lily. The seascape before them is presented as being in some way necessary to them and interpreted according to their desire for renewal. In the vivid depiction of the alternating colours and aspects of the sea there is a strong symbolic suggestion of the sea's ability to contain dual and conflicting powers, whose very contradictions stimulate the watchers. The dash of white water against the great black rock echoes this theme of restrained duality, while at the same time hinting at images previously used to describe Mr and Mrs Ramsay. In the second paragraph there is an emotional movement from 'common hilarity' at the exhilaration of the scene to 'some sadness' because something was finished and because the seascape bore witness to the contrast between man's short life and the permanence of nature. This second paragraph anticipates the development of the novel: the temporarily becalmed boat foreshadows the Ramsays' boat in Part III, the movement from exhilaration to sadness corresponds to a similar movement in the novel, the suddenly sinister quality of the landscape suggests the hostility of nature in Part II, and the indefinite figure of 'the gazer', here associated with Lily the artist, will reappear significantly in Part II.

The second passage, taken from 'Time Passes', provides a sharp contrast, in that the observations are unconnected to any of the novel's characters but are attributed to 'those who had gone to pace the beach'. More subtly, those actions concerning Andrew's death are related by an omniscient narrator and separated by style and parentheses from the description of the sea, as if the world of nature and the world of man had completely separated. The first details of the seascape presented here are banal and colourless, and the omniscient narrator directs the reader's attention to its hidden, threatening qualities. The difference between the outward appearance of the seascape and its secret ferocity moves from the level of outward appearance to a level of abstract philosophical language, culminating in a direct rejection of nature as a benevolent mirror of human optimism.

Symbolic structure

When we speak of the structure of a novel, a play or a poem, we mean that ingredient of a work of literature which organises and unifies all its elements, as the human skeleton provides a 'structure' for the body, or a framework of steel girders provides a 'structure' for a modern skyscraper. In the nineteenth-century novel, structure usually consisted of plot, in the sense of story or development of character, or a combination of the two. Plot provided the pretext for introducing a new character, describing a particular scene, reporting certain conversations. The structure of such novels had a clear beginning, middle and end, based on the development of plot.

The term 'symbolic structure' is, therefore, ambivalent, since it can refer to a structure which is symbolic in the sense that the external action (plot) of *To the Lighthouse* is clearly symbolic, or it can indicate that the very structure of the novel is based on the development of symbols, on the kind of growth in a symbol's meaning which we have observed is an integral characteristic of *To the Lighthouse*.

The obvious external structure of *To the Lighthouse* depends on the resolution of whether or not the Ramsays will visit the lighthouse, and on the development of various characters to the point where a visit to the lighthouse is possible. It seems obvious, however, that this plot or structure will not, of itself, provide the main focus for the reader's interest. In selecting the story of a journey as a mainspring of action in *To the Lighthouse*, Virginia Woolf was drawing upon a richly suggestive tradition in Western literature whose roots extend to the Arthurian legends and the pilgrimage stories of the Middle Ages: so the reader of *To the Lighthouse* with any experience of this tradition will readily see the plot of the novel in a symbolic light.

The voyage of Mr Ramsay and his children to the lighthouse is clearly symbolic; for Lily, the artist-observer, it is also a journey of spiritual and aesthetic discovery. To reach the final achievement of the arrival at the lighthouse in the physical and moral sense, all these characters undergo internal change and growth, parallel to the external progress of their respective journeys. The novel's structure, in the sense of story and character development, is clearly symbolical. If we examine the last two sections of the novel, it is evident that narrative and symbolic meanings are so completely intertwined that all the action and dialogue can be read as referring to both the interior and exterior journeys.

The impregnation of external character and action with symbolic meaning is by no means revolutionary. In one sense all great art is symbolic for it points towards deeper, more universal truths than its surface meaning. Many travel and adventure novels are clearly intended to suggest spiritual growth (for example, Joseph Conrad's *Heart of Darkness*) but in *To the Lighthouse* another kind of symbolic structure exists, based on the reader's increasing perception of wider and wider areas of significance associated with symbols. Such development is usually associated with poetry rather than the novel, and there are many critics who believe that *To the Lighthouse* fails as a novel because of its reliance on a network of symbols to carry the main meaning. Whether or not you take this viewpoint will depend on your definition of the novel and your understanding of the novel's limitations.

Part 5

Suggestions for further reading

The text

The most widely available text of Virginia Woolf's *To the Lighthouse*, and the one used in the preparation of these Notes, is the paperback edition published by Triad/Panther, London 1977. In the U.S.A. a paperback edition of the novel is published by Harcourt Brace Janovich.

Autobiographical and biographical material

Because of the autobiographical nature of *To the Lighthouse*, the following are of particular interest:

ANNAN, NOEL GILROY: *Leslie Stephen: His Thought and Character in Relation to his Time*, MacGibbon & Kee, London, 1952.

BELL, QUENTIN: *Virginia Woolf, A Biography*, Hogarth Press, London, 1972.

Bloomsbury, Weidenfeld & Nicolson, London, 1968.

WOOLF, LEONARD: *Autobiography*, 5 vols., Hogarth Press, London, 1960–7.

WOOLF, VIRGINIA: *The Letters of Virginia Woolf*, ed. Nigel Nicolson, Hogarth Press, London, 1975–7.

A Writer's Diary, ed. Leonard Woolf, Hogarth Press, London, 1953.

Moments of Being: Unpublished Autobiographical Writings, ed. Jeanne Schulkind, Sussex University Press, Sussex, 1976.

Critical studies

BEJA, MORRIS (ED.): *Virginia Woolf. To the Lighthouse: A Casebook*, Macmillan, London, 1970. An excellent selection of some of the best criticism of *To the Lighthouse*.

MCNICHOL, STELLA: *Virginia Woolf. To the Lighthouse*. Edward Arnold, London, 1971. This short survey of *To the Lighthouse* is particularly good for its discussion of symbolism and characterisation.

The author of these notes

ELIZABETH GROVE-WHITE was educated at Trinity College, Dublin. She lectured there for two years and then went to Canada, where she has taught in Victoria College, University of Toronto. At present she is preparing to publish a study of Virginia Woolf's criticism.

The first 150 titles

		Series number
CHINUA ACHEBE	*A Man of the People*	(116)
	Arrow of God	(92)
	Things Fall Apart	(96)
ELECHI AMADI	*The Concubine*	(139)
JANE AUSTEN	*Emma*	(142)
	Northanger Abbey	(1)
	Persuasion	(69)
	Pride and Prejudice	(62)
	Sense and Sensibility	(91)
SAMUEL BECKETT	*Waiting for Godot*	(115)
SAUL BELLOW	*Henderson, The Rain King*	(146)
ARNOLD BENNETT	*Anna of the Five Towns*	(144)
ROBERT BOLT	*A Man For All Seasons*	(51)
CHARLOTTE BRONTË	*Jane Eyre*	(21)
EMILY BRONTË	*Wuthering Heights*	(43)
JOHN BUCHAN	*The Thirty-Nine Steps*	(89)
ALBERT CAMUS	*L'Etranger (The Outsider)*	(46)
GEOFFREY CHAUCER	*Prologue to the Canterbury Tales*	(30)
	The Franklin's Tale	(78)
	The Knight's Tale	(97)
	The Nun's Priest's Tale	(16)
	The Pardoner's Tale	(50)
	The Wife of Bath's Tale	(109)
SIR ARTHUR CONAN DOYLE	*The Hound of the Baskervilles*	(53)
JOSEPH CONRAD	*Lord Jim*	(150)
	Nostromo	(68)
	Youth and *Typhoon*	(100)
DANIEL DEFOE	*Robinson Crusoe*	(28)
CHARLES DICKENS	*A Tale of Two Cities*	(70)
	David Copperfield	(9)
	Great Expectations	(66)
	Oliver Twist	(101)
	The Pickwick Papers	(110)
GEORGE ELIOT	*Adam Bede*	(14)
	Silas Marner	(98)
	The Mill on the Floss	(29)
T. S. ELIOT	*Murder in the Cathedral*	(149)
	The Waste Land	(45)
WILLIAM FAULKNER	*Absalom, Absalom!*	(124)
	As I Lay Dying	(44)
	The Sound and the Fury	(136)
HENRY FIELDING	*Joseph Andrews*	(105)
	Tom Jones	(113)
F. SCOTT FITZGERALD	*The Great Gatsby*	(8)

		Series number
ATHOL FUGARD	*Selected Plays*	(63)
MRS GASKELL	*North and South*	(60)
WILLIAM GOLDING	*Lord of the Flies*	(77)
OLIVER GOLDSMITH	*She Stoops to Conquer*	(71)
	The Vicar of Wakefield	(79)
THOMAS HARDY	*Jude the Obscure*	(6)
	Tess of the D'Urbervilles	(80)
	The Mayor of Casterbridge	(39)
	The Return of the Native	(20)
	The Trumpet Major	(74)
	Under the Greenwood Tree	(129)
L. P. HARTLEY	*The Go-Between*	(36)
	The Shrimp and the Anemone	(123)
NATHANIEL HAWTHORNE	*The Scarlet Letter*	(134)
ERNEST HEMINGWAY	*A Farewell to Arms*	(145)
	For Whom the Bell Tolls	(95)
	The Old Man and the Sea	(11)
HERMANN HESSE	*Steppenwolf*	(135)
ANTHONY HOPE	*The Prisoner of Zenda*	(88)
RICHARD HUGHES	*A High Wind in Jamaica*	(17)
THOMAS HUGHES	*Tom Brown's Schooldays*	(2)
HENRIK IBSEN	*A Doll's House*	(85)
	Ghosts	(131)
HENRY JAMES	*Daisy Miller*	(147)
	The Europeans	(120)
	The Portrait of a Lady	(117)
	The Turn of the Screw	(27)
SAMUEL JOHNSON	*Rasselas*	(137)
BEN JONSON	*The Alchemist*	(102)
	Volpone	(15)
RUDYARD KIPLING	*Kim*	(114)
D. H. LAWRENCE	*Sons and Lovers*	(24)
	The Rainbow	(59)
	Women in Love	(143)
HARPER LEE	*To Kill a Mocking-Bird*	(125)
CHRISTOPHER MARLOWE	*Doctor Faustus*	(127)
SOMERSET MAUGHAM	*Selected Short Stories*	(38)
HERMAN MELVILLE	*Billy Budd*	(10)
	Moby Dick	(126)
ARTHUR MILLER	*Death of a Salesman*	(32)
	The Crucible	(3)
JOHN MILTON	*Paradise Lost I & II*	(94)
	Paradise Lost IV & IX	(87)
SEAN O'CASEY	*Juno and the Paycock*	(112)
EUGENE O'NEILL	*Mourning Becomes Electra*	(130)
GEORGE ORWELL	*Animal Farm*	(37)
	Nineteen Eighty-four	(67)
JOHN OSBORNE	*Look Back in Anger*	(128)
HAROLD PINTER	*The Birthday Party*	(25)
	The Caretaker	(106)
THOMAS PYNCHON	*The Crying of Lot 49*	(148)

		Series number
J. D. SALINGER	*The Catcher in the Rye*	(31)
SIR WALTER SCOTT	*Ivanhoe*	(58)
	Quentin Durward	(54)
	The Heart of Midlothian	(141)
	Waverley	(122)
WILLIAM SHAKESPEARE	*A Midsummer Night's Dream*	(26)
	Antony and Cleopatra	(82)
	As You Like It	(108)
	Coriolanus	(35)
	Cymbeline	(93)
	Hamlet	(84)
	Henry IV Part I	(83)
	Henry IV Part II	(140)
	Henry V	(40)
	Julius Caesar	(13)
	King Lear	(18)
	Love's Labour's Lost	(72)
	Macbeth	(4)
	Measure for Measure	(33)
	Much Ado About Nothing	(73)
	Othello	(34)
	Richard II	(41)
	Richard III	(119)
	Romeo and Juliet	(64)
	The Merchant of Venice	(107)
	The Taming of the Shrew	(118)
	The Tempest	(22)
	The Winter's Tale	(65)
	Troilus and Cressida	(47)
	Twelfth Night	(42)
GEORGE BERNARD SHAW	*Androcles and the Lion*	(56)
	Arms and the Man	(12)
	Caesar and Cleopatra	(57)
	Pygmalion	(5)
RICHARD BRINSLEY SHERIDAN	*The School for Scandal*	(55)
	The Rivals	(104)
WOLE SOYINKA	*The Road*	(133)
JOHN STEINBECK	*Of Mice and Men*	(23)
	The Grapes of Wrath	(7)
	The Pearl	(99)
ROBERT LOUIS STEVENSON	*Kidnapped*	(90)
	Treasure Island	(48)
	Dr Jekyll and Mr Hyde	(132)
JONATHAN SWIFT	*Gulliver's Travels*	(61)
JOHN MILLINGTON SYNGE	*The Playboy of the Western World*	(111)
W. M. THACKERAY	*Vanity Fair*	(19)
J. R. R. TOLKIEN	*The Hobbit*	(121)
MARK TWAIN	*Huckleberry Finn*	(49)
	Tom Sawyer	(76)
VOLTAIRE	*Candide*	(81)
H. G. WELLS	*The History of Mr Polly*	(86)
	The Invisible Man	(52)
	The War of the Worlds	(103)
OSCAR WILDE	*The Importance of Being Earnest*	(75)